Octopus

Animal
Series editor: Jonathan Burt

Already published

Ant Charlotte Sleigh · *Ape* John Sorenson · *Bear* Robert E. Bieder · *Bee* Claire Preston
Camel Robert Irwin · *Cat* Katharine M. Rogers · *Chicken* Annie Potts · *Cockroach* Marion Copeland
Cow Hannah Velten · *Crocodile* Dan Wylie · *Crow* Boria Sax · *Deer* John Fletcher · *Dog* Susan McHugh
Dolphin Alan Rauch · *Donkey* Jill Bough · *Duck* Victoria de Rijke · *Eel* Richard Schweid
Elephant Dan Wylie · *Falcon* Helen Macdonald · *Fly* Steven Connor · *Fox* Martin Wallen
Frog Charlotte Sleigh · *Giraffe* Edgar Williams · *Gorilla* Ted Gott and Kathryn Weir
Hare Simon Carnell · *Horse* Elaine Walker · *Hyena* Mikita Brottman · *Kangaroo* John Simons
Leech Robert G. W. Kirk and Neil Pemberton · *Lion* Deirdre Jackson · *Lobster* Richard J. King
Monkey Desmond Morris · *Moose* Kevin Jackson · *Mosquito* Richard Jones · *Octopus* Richard Schweid
Ostrich Edgar Williams · *Otter* Daniel Allen · *Owl* Desmond Morris · *Oyster* Rebecca Stott
Parrot Paul Carter · *Peacock* Christine E. Jackson · *Penguin* Stephen Martin · *Pig* Brett Mizelle
Pigeon Barbara Allen · *Rabbit* Victoria Dickenson · *Rat* Jonathan Burt · *Rhinoceros* Kelly Enright
Salmon Peter Coates · *Shark* Dean Crawford · *Snail* Peter Williams · *Snake* Drake Stutesman
Sparrow Kim Todd · *Spider* Katja and Sergiusz Michalski · *Swan* Peter Young · *Tiger* Susie Green
Tortoise Peter Young · *Trout* James Owen · *Vulture* Thom van Dooren · *Whale* Joe Roman
Wolf Garry Marvin

Octopus

Richard Schweid

REAKTION BOOKS

Published by
REAKTION BOOKS LTD
33 Great Sutton Street
London EC1V 0DX, UK
www.reaktionbooks.co.uk

First published 2014
Copyright © Richard Schweid 2014

All rights reserved

No part of this publication may be reproduced, stored in a retrieval system or transmitted, in any form or by any means, electronic, mechanical, photocopying, recording or otherwise without the prior permission of the publishers

Printed and bound in China by C&C Offset Printing Co., Ltd

A catalogue record for this book is available from the British Library

ISBN 978 1 78023 177 8

Contents

1 Octopus Body 7
2 Octopus Brain 47
3 Octopus Mind 64
4 Octopus Fishing, Farming and Marketing 80
5 Octopus Cuisine 105
6 Octopus Iconography 126
7 Octopus Keeping 155
   Timeline 176
   References 179
   Select Bibliography 189
   Associations and Websites 191
   Acknowledgements 192
   Photo Acknowledgements 193
   Index 195

1 Octopus Body

When you watch an octopus, an octopus watches you back. A surprising degree of unanimity on this point exists among people who spend a lot of time observing octopuses (the generally accepted plural spelling for *octopus*). They all agree that when they do so, the animals closely observe them in turn. Gazing for any length of time at an octopus, particularly *Octopus vulgaris*, the common octopus – the species most Europeans, Americans and Asians know – leads to the inescapable conclusion that the animal is looking back, and is somehow thinking about what it is seeing. Jacques Cousteau, who encountered thousands of octopuses during his lifetime of diving, wrote in his book *Octopus and Squid: The Soft Intelligence* (1973) that an undersea diver who encounters an octopus immediately senses something unusually responsive in its gaze: 'One has the sensation of lucidity, of a look much more expressive than that of any fish, or even any marine mammal.'[1]

No researcher working with octopuses remains oblivious to the fact that he or she is under observation, no matter how rigorous and rational their scientific approach. Roger Hanlon, a senior scientist at the Marine Biological Laboratory in Woods Hole, Massachusetts, has been working with octopuses since 1968. He is widely considered to be among the most judicious and careful of current octopus researchers, and his book *Cephalopod Behavior*

(1996) is still the standard reference work in the field. Even he writes that there is something disconcerting about being regarded by an octopus: 'anyone who has seen an octopus in an aquarium will have had the uncanny impression of being carefully watched.'[2] And Martin J. Wells, a prominent twentieth-century British octopus researcher and the grandson of H. G. Wells,

Mosaic from a ruin at Pompeii.

Octopus in a fresco in Voroneț monastery, Romania, mid-16th century.

wrote: 'Anyone watching an octopus for the first time is bound to notice that he is being observed.'[3]

That, however, is where the unanimity of opinions about what goes on in an octopus's brain ends. As we shall see, while some researchers recently have posited that octopuses have complex minds and astounding mental capacities, others are not so sure. What *is* certain is that octopuses have been observing humans, and vice versa, for a long time. The record is ancient: pottery from the Middle and Late Minoan periods (*c.* 2000–1000 BCE) often features images of octopuses and other marine creatures, and it also occurs as an Egyptian hieroglyph.[4]

The octopus itself is an ancient invertebrate marine animal. Like their close relatives, squids and cuttlefishes, octopuses

Scuba divers regularly report handling octopuses.

François-Nicolas Chifflart, 'The Monster', engraving for an 1869 edition of Victor Hugo's *Toilers of the Sea*.

belong to the cephalopodan class of coleoid molluscs. The name is derived from the Greek words *kephale* and *podus*, meaning 'head-footed', and refers to the fact that the animal's arms are directly connected to its head. The class consists of squids, cuttlefishes and octopuses along with nautiluses, the only group of the four to have shells.

Currently some 100 species are identified as members of the genus *Octopus*, and another 200 belong to other genera. Octopuses live in all the world's oceans at a variety of depths. The Hawaiian day octopus (*Octopus cyanea*) lives in shallow tide pools, while the spoon-armed octopus (*Bathypolypus arcticus*) can be found on the dark Atlantic Ocean floor at 800 m (0.5 miles) deep. Octopuses also come in all sizes. At the small end of the scale is the tiny Atlantic pygmy octopus (*Octopus joubini*), with a mantle length of 4.5 cm (1.8 in) and arms of 9 cm (3.5 in), or the even smaller California Lilliput octopus, *Octopus micropyrsus*, which is about 2 cm across, while the giant Pacific octopus (*Enteroctopus dofleini*) can weigh over 45 kg (100 lb) and measure well over 6 m (20 ft) between the tips of its arms. Reproductive

Octopus in the waters of the Channel Islands.

Newly discovered Purple octopus, found in 2010 off Canada's Atlantic coast.

strategies differ, even among close relatives. With the exception of the Mediterranean's football octopus (*Ocythoe tuberculata*), which hatches its eggs internally and gives birth to live young, all other octopuses are oviparous, hatching their eggs externally. The Verrill's two-spot octopus (*Octopus bimaculatus*), which lives on rocky reefs from California to Panama, produces 20,000 tiny eggs at a time, while the closely related California two-spot octopus (*Octopus bimaculoides*) opts for 800 large eggs. While all octopuses use some measure of camouflage for defence, none of them equal the ingenuity of the mimic octopus (*Thaumoctopus mimicus*) found in Southeast Asian waters, which buries six of its arms in the sand and uses the other two to mimic the movement and colour of the yellow-and-black-banded venomous sea snake, frightening away predators.

In primeval times, when cephalopods thrived and multiplied, the class was even more diverse. Those relatively few members living today are the descendants of an ancient lineage. Some of the oldest fossils on record, dating back more than 350 million years, are of long-extinct cephalopods. Those ancient shelled creatures were members of more than 3,000 species which ranged in size from 6 to 460 cm long (2.5 in to 15 ft).[5]

Among octopus researchers there is general agreement that during the Silurian period (some 420 million years ago), the cephalopods had it relatively easy. They had shells and lived close to the coasts, greatly outnumbering what fish there were around them. However, this gradually changed. The Devonian period that followed is often called the Age of Fish because piscine species became so abundant at that time: they were present in far greater numbers and with more sophisticated hunting skills than ever before. This had two negative results for cephalopods: it reduced the amount of prey for them to hunt, and it increased the number of potential predators that would hunt for them. Cephalopods needed to increase their range and their manoeuvrability, and over the course of the next 100 million years or so they gradually internalized and eliminated their shells so they could take to deeper water. Aside from the nautilus, all cephalopods have soft bodies, and are mainstays in the diets of many marine animals larger than they are. In compensation for the lack of a shell, cephalopods are the only molluscs that have a brain. While it is not as complex as the mammalian brain, an octopus's body-to-brain weight ratio far exceeds that of other invertebrates.

Their evolutionary history bears a striking resemblance to our own, noted Martin J. Wells:

There is . . . a haunting similarity in the history of *Octopus* and ourselves. Both of us have evolved from groups obliged to spend a period in the wilderness, eking out a peripheral existence while other animals, temporarily better adapted, dominated the more desirable habitats. The teleost fish and the great reptiles respectively forced upon us a way of life that depended upon adaptability rather than armour, a capacity to know when to run and how to detect trouble in the making that has eventually placed the coleoids and the mammal in a unique position with respect to their invertebrate and vertebrate competitors.[6]

Early on, the octopus's amazing survival strategies drew peoples' attention. The Greeks noted its remarkable ability to

Reef octopus.

camouflage itself. As early as the sixth century BCE, noted Henry Lee, a naturalist and director of the Brighton Aquarium who wrote *The Octopus* in 1875, the Greek poet Theognis of Megara wrote of the octopus's amazing ability to blend in:

> Remark the tricks of that most wary polypus [octopus]
> Who always seems of the same colour and hue
> As is the rock on which he lies . . .

Lee also cited another Greek writer, Clearchus of Soli from around 300 BCE, who passed along this advice to his offspring:

> My son, my excellent Amphilocus,
> Copy the shrewd device o' the polypus,
> And make yourself as like as possible,
> To those whose land you chance to visit.[7]

The motives for the camouflage of the octopus were occasionally called into question by such writers as the Roman natural historian Claudius Aelianus, who wrote at the turn of the third century CE, 'Mischief and craft are plainly seen to be the characteristics of this creature.'[8]

Aristotle, the world's first great naturalist, wrote about octopus in his *History of Animals* around 350 BCE. He described them as neat and thrifty in their habits:

> It lays up stores in its nest and, after eating up all that is edible, it ejects the shells and sheaths of crabs and shellfish, and the skeletons of little fishes. It seeks its prey by so changing its colour as to render it like the colour of the stones adjacent to it; it does so also when alarmed.[9]

The Pearl Necklace by the contemporary Italian artist Benedetta Bonichi, 2002.

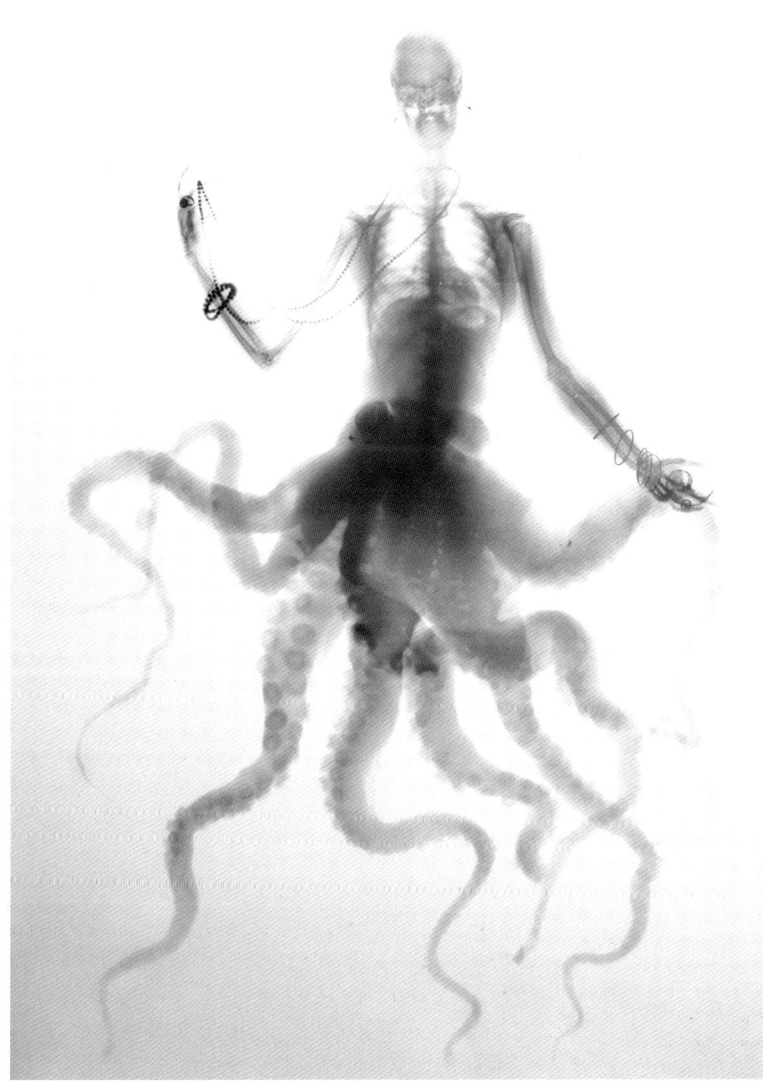

The subtle colours and patterns that an octopus is able to project almost instantly on its skin are produced by its chromatophores, pigment cells that reflect light and are used both for camouflage and to communicate with other octopuses. These cells are capable of changing pigmentation rapidly, as well as reorienting their reflective plates.

The noted behavioural evolutionary biologist Martin Moynihan found 33 different patterns used again and again by Caribbean reef squid, some of which, he posited, conveyed specific messages among them. Of course, camouflage is one thing and communication another. However, it seemed possible to Moynihan that in addition to serving as a survival strategy for an animal without the protection of a shell, the numerous and subtle colour changes were a language that one cephalopod uses to communicate with another. 'The various postures, movements, and chromatophore

Colour changing allows this octopus to look like a flounder.

Greek vase, c. 1100 BCE.

arrangements involved in . . . communication are comparable to the phonemes or morphemes of human language', he wrote in 1985.[10]

What is certain is that when they are used for camouflage purposes, the chromatophores serve as a first line of defence. Octopuses move quickly, but cannot do so for long. When faced with a threat they prefer to disappear rather than flee, and are able to do so in the blink of an eye, camouflaging themselves to match their surroundings with a speed unmatched by any other animal.

Octopus blood is blue because it contains haemocyanin, a compound which contains copper. Two of an octopus's hearts are gill hearts used to pump the blue blood through the gills, while the other, the systemic heart, pumps it through the body. Cephalopod blood can only transport about one-third as much oxygen as fish blood. Octopuses that are fleeing, or pursuing, run into oxygen debt quite rapidly.[11] A frightened octopus will propel itself at high speed but cannot keep going for long.

For all its survival strategies and its vaunted intelligence, the octopus has many potential predators that treat it first and foremost as a tasty meal. These include not only big fish like whales and dolphins, but also humans. *Octopus vulgaris* has long been a favourite food of *Homo sapiens* in many places around the globe. More than 100 million lb (45.5 million kg) a year of the common octopus are taken out of the world's seas and oceans. With so many marine predators, and such a big global market for octopus around the world, the only reason the animal is not on a rapid road to extinction is because it is so prolific. A female common

Pacific octopus.

octopus will only ever lay one clutch of eggs in her lifetime, but she will lay over 100,000 of them.

O. vulgaris, camouflaged.

Octopus sex and reproduction do not sound particularly attractive. Most octopuses copulate only once in their lifetimes, and both males and females die shortly afterwards: the wages of octopus sex are death. The male octopus's third arm from its right eye is called a hectocotylus, and is reserved for sex. In fact the best way to determine the gender of an octopus is by inspecting this arm to determine whether it has the peripheral canal that carries the packet of sperm (or spermataphore). If not, you're looking at a female.

The hectocotylus's specific and only function is copulation. At the end of this arm is the male octopus's penis. The tip of the hectocotylus is inserted into the oviduct of the female, which is located in her mantle. In some species of octopus, although not the common octopus, the hectocotylus breaks off and remains lodged in the oviduct. It was this sight that caused Georges Cuvier

An Italian dish of octopus stewed in wine and tomatoes.

in 1829 to coin the name 'hectocotylus' for what he assumed was a parasite in the mantle of a female argonaut he was examining. It was no parasite, but the male's reproductive organ; the name stuck.

Curiously Aristotle almost got it right, but seemed unable to believe in such a curious form of copulation:

> They unite at the mouth through an interlacing of their tentacles. When, then, the octopus rests its so-called head against the ground and spreads abroad its tentacles, the other sex fits into the outspreading of these tentacles, and the two sexes then bring their suckers into mutual connection.

Some assert that the male has a kind of penis in one of his tentacles, the one in which are the largest suckers, and they further assert that the organ is tendinous in character, growing attached right up to the middle of the tentacle, and that the latter enables it to enter the nostril or funnel of the female.[12]

Once the hectocotylus is in place for copulation, the two octopuses may stay connected for an hour or so as the spermatophore is transferred. They remain immobile and apparently unmoved by the experience, their heartbeats as steady as when they are resting. This apparent lack of ardour makes physiological sense, according to researchers, who point to the fact that octopus blood is oxygen-poor.

Octopuses tire easily. It takes a while to move that sperm packet down the hectocotylus, and there is no reason to waste energy by getting all excited. Once the transfer is accomplished, no further relationship between the female and the male takes

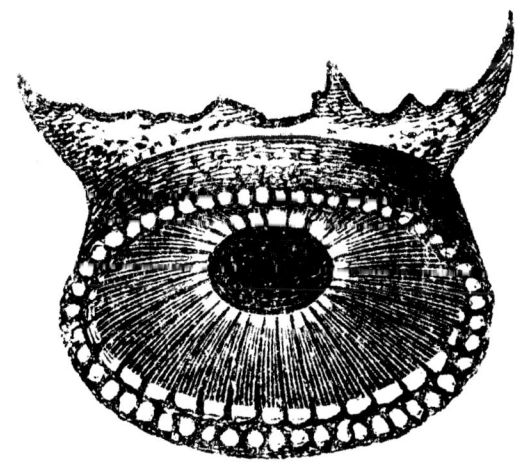

Sucker of the *O. vulgaris*.

Octopus, 16th century, Italian, artist unknown.

place. The female retains the spermatophore in her body until her eggs mature, at which point she fertilizes them.

A gravid (pregnant) female finds a sheltered, dim space, and a couple of weeks may pass before she produces her eggs. Once begun, the process can take as long as five days. When the clusters of eggs are extruded, she hangs them in long strings from the ceiling or walls of her shelter. The eggs need constant fanning to keep them clean, and a female spends her days tending the eggs, keeping them clean with jets of water. Once she has strung her eggs and begun tending to them she will stop eating, and shortly after they hatch out she will die.

An octopus is doomed to a woefully short life of a couple of years at most before senescence, or ageing, occurs. In octopuses this is an odd, extreme dimming of the will to survive until the light just goes out. Senescence occurs in the days and weeks following copulation. The female hangs her clusters of eggs and stops eating or going out, living only long enough to tend the eggs. She is so weak that when they finally hatch she succumbs to death almost immediately. At least, an observer might posit, the female's behaviour has some rationale: if she goes out to hunt she could get eaten and not come back to tend the eggs, so in an example of extreme maternal sacrifice she keeps the eggs clean and safe while she wastes away.

The male, who has absolutely nothing to do with the female or the eggs after copulation, and is to all appearances free to carry on living as he did before mating, also enters into senescence. He may live for another a couple of months, and he may even pass a second spermataphore to another female, but it's a short-lived healthiness. Soon he stops hunting, eating only what passes close enough for him not to be able to ignore it, and loses weight rapidly. He spends most of his time exposed, outside his den. Worse, he gradually loses coordination and camouflage ability, and his skin develops lesions. As an octopus loses weight its eyes remain the same size, so they seem to bulge out in horror at what lies just ahead. All the characteristics and behaviours that keep an octopus alive disappear, and death follows shortly afterwards.

In an intriguing experiment by psychologist Jerome Wodinsky from Brandeis University, octopuses that had their optic glands removed were shown to have increased longevity. In an article published in *Science* in 1977, Wodinsky noted that females that had undergone this procedure stopped tending their eggs and began eating heartily once again. The species of octopus he used, *Octopus hummelincki*, also called the bumblebee octopus or Caribbean two-spot, hunts snails and eats them by boring holes into their shells, injecting a secretion and pulling out the weakened snail. Once an *O. hummelincki* female begins to brood her eggs, she stops this behaviour, and simply uses force to pull the snail's

A female octopus guarding her eggs.

Octopus eggs in close-up.

body from its shell when she encounters one, eating less and less until the eggs hatch and she dies. Once her optic glands are removed, however, she reverts to the boring technique and eats heartily. While the longest-lived female that had not been operated on made it to 51 days after laying eggs, those that had the glands removed lived much longer – up to nine months.[13]

Of course, senescence is also what happens to human beings as we age past our ideal reproductive years: our appetites are reduced, the acuity of our senses diminishes and our own survival skills gradually disappear as we approach our inevitable ends. Octopuses in the throes of senescence can become so disoriented that they climb out of the water on to beaches, resembling the way a person with dementia may wander off without taking the least precaution.

When the eggs so zealously guarded by the female finally hatch after six weeks or so, the larvae behave in different ways depending on the species. In *O. vulgaris*, for instance, the larvae are planktonic and spend almost two months drifting at midlevel in the water column before finally sinking to the bottom,

Small octopus on a rock.

27

where the octopuses will pass the rest of their lives. Larvae of *Octopus maya*, on the other hand, a species closely related to the common octopus and found in abundance off Mexico's Yucatán coast, are benthic (living at the sea bottom). They bypass the drifting phase and go straight to the bottom after hatching. Another difference between these two species is the number of eggs the female extrudes. In the common octopus, which suffers a high mortality rate among larvae eaten while they drift helplessly in the water column, the female lays upwards of 100,000 eggs, but a female Mayan octopus will only produce about 4,000 eggs. Once these hatch, the *O. maya* larvae immediately go to the sea bed, where they begin hunting tiny live prey and displaying the same variety of evasion tactics that are in an adult octopus's repertoire. Even in their first weeks of life, for instance, they squirt out a thin thread of ink and jet away when threatened.

At first blush an adult octopus might not seem to need much in the way of evasion tactics. It is a pretty formidable foe even for a dolphin or moray eel, two animals that relentlessly prey on octopus. With eight strong arms lined with powerful, sensitive suckers, a sharp beak and poisonous saliva, an octopus seems designed to be an aggressive opponent. In reality, it prefers fleeing to fighting. When Ringo Starr sang The Beatles's song 'Octopus's Garden', about being happy and safe living with an octopus under the sea, he was right on the mark.

The common octopus likes nothing better than to find an inviting den, strew some rocks and clam shells in front of it and curl up inside, occasionally coming out in search of food. An octopus is such a domestic creature, such a homebody, that octopus fishermen do not need bait to catch them – they simply drop a line of empty clay pots, about the size of 2-litre (0.5 gallon) jugs, to rest on the sandy bottom, each an attractive dwelling in the eyes of an octopus. They move right in, night after night, and all the

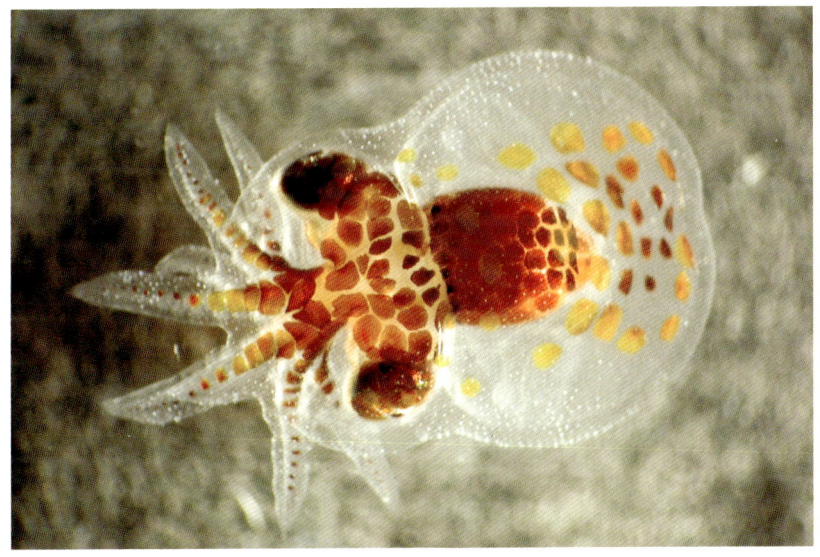

Octopus larva drifting during its planktonic stage.

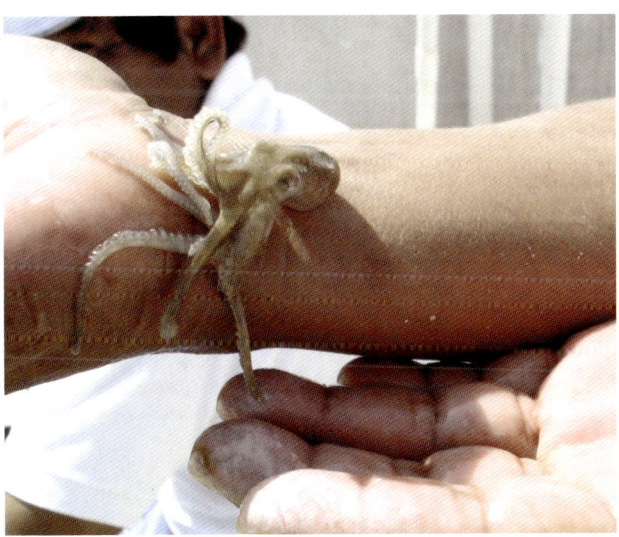

Baby *Octopus maya*.

A dolphin about to gobble up an octopus, one of its favourite meals.

fisherman has to do is pull them up in the morning. Once curled up inside a clay pot, an octopus will usually refuse to leave, even when its new home is hauled up to a boat above. This method of fishing has been used across the globe for millennia. It was used in the Mediterranean by the Romans, who got it from the Greeks, who are thought to have learned it from the Egyptians. Japanese octopus fishermen have caught them in the same way since time immemorial.

Despite being a reclusive stay-at-home, the octopus is by no means a pacifist. Like most living creatures, including humans, at different times an octopus can be both pursuer and prey. An adult octopus is an accomplished hunter, and woe unto the creature on which it sets its sights. However, an octopus is also a delectable mouthful of protein, and for some species – such as moray eels, dolphins and sharks – it is the preferred dish on life's menu. Frank Lane, in *Kingdom of the Octopus* (1960), describes how moray eels will sometimes eat an octopus arm by arm, tearing each loose from the body one by one.

> Grasping an arm in its vice-like jaws, the eel stretches its body full length and then spins itself round and round until the arm is twisted off. It is then swallowed, and unless the octopus has managed to escape during this slight pause, the eel continues to eat it an arm at a time.[14]

Octopuses have developed some responses to threats that are frequently effective. Their first choice is to pass unnoticed. If that doesn't work, they go into flight mode, squirting out a cloud of ink from a special ink sac, a small organ between the gills. Lane wrote that the ink is so strong that it can be extracted from cephalopod fossils that are over 100 million years old and still be used to write or draw.[15] (He also notes that the ink used by Georges Cuvier to illustrate his work on the Mollusca was what he had collected while dissecting cephalopods.[16]) The octopus expels ink through its funnel, then sucks in water through it and squirts it out hard, jetting away behind the cloud of ink. The rubbery membrane connecting its arms also contracts to draw water into

Charles Livingston Bull (1874–1932), drawing of an octopus ensnaring a fish.

An octopus tucked inside its home.

Octopus pots in southern Portugal; such traps are used around the world.

the gills, where oxygen is extracted for the blood. When the water has been filtered through the gills, it is expelled by the siphon. If done with force, this expulsion of water can also serve to rapidly propel an octopus.

Almost all the squids, cuttlefishes and octopuses in the world use ink as a defence. The ink is dense – like the visual equivalent of a skunk's smell – and is impossible to get out of clothing, as many have found out over the centuries. The natural reaction when that ink explodes in a cloud in front of you is to move back, giving the octopus time to disappear behind it. Marine biologist Roger Hanlon writes:

> Although the ink is usually taken to act as a visual screen it may also act to block olfactory or taste receptors. Moray eels attacking octopuses and teleost fishes attacking young cuttlefish or reef squids all react to a large cloud of ink by hesitating and shaking their heads for several moments.[17]

The discharging of its ink sac is an involuntary muscular reaction that is not always to an octopus's advantage. If an animal is being transported in a bucket, say, and inks, its gills may be coated with the dense liquid and it may suffocate. The same thing can happen if an octopus inks in a home aquarium.

If nothing else works to allow an octopus to escape being eaten, it may be able to satisfy its attacker by giving up an arm. As many lizards can do with their tails, an octopus can shed an arm to escape. All of an octopus's arms, apart from the male's hectocotyl, are capable of regeneration. Some older octopus fishermen in the Mediterranean insist that the animal eats its own arms when it gets hungry, and that's why they occasionally catch one with only seven arms, or an eighth arm that's much shorter than the rest. In fact, say marine biologists, if an octopus

A swimming octopus is a streamlined thing of beauty.

devours its own arm it is a signal that the animal is extremely stressed.

Its ability to regenerate is by no means the only impressive thing about an octopus's arm. Composed of densely packed muscle and nerve fibres, it is remarkably flexible. An international group of researchers from Italy, Israel, Greece, Switzerland and the UK is working on a project to integrate the design of an octopus arm with a robotic appendage. In a grant proposal to the EU, they wrote:

> The octopus is the ideal animal model for studying the generation and control of the movements of flexible arms. The knowledge thus gained is of immense relevance to the field of biologically inspired robotics. Data already obtained on the octopus' outstandingly efficient nervous and muscular

control of its eight flexible arms ... can inspire the design and control of flexible robotic arms.[18]

Each arm has about 200 suckers which have tremendous gripping power, as anyone who has ever tried to pull an octopus's arm loose from something will testify. Each sucker has some 10,000 receptor cells. Some are mechanoreceptors, which perceive by touch, sending the information they gather directly to the learning centre in the brain. It has been shown in the laboratory that octopuses can easily learn to discriminate between textures like rough, smooth and many stages in between.[19] The sucker's chemoreceptor cells deal with what we think of as smell and taste. These same suckers that can exert tremendous pressure and can hold on to something with surprising strength are highly sensitive sense receptors. Octopuses can detect trace amounts of substances like quinine, hydrochloric acid or sucrose in concentrations up to 1,000 times smaller than those to which humans respond.[20]

An octopus perceives the world through its suckers, but also through its eyes. Just looking at an octopus's bulging eyes gives us a clue that they play a large role in the animal's life, and so it is. Octopuses can distinguish between degrees of brightness and size, between horizontal and vertical, and between distinct geometrical forms, all of which are usually thought of as vertebrate traits.

One visual trait that they apparently cannot appreciate is colour, and it is generally held that octopuses are colour-blind. Wells reviewed ten experiments on the subject, done between 1910 and 1968, 60 per cent of which definitely concluded that octopuses don't see colours. He admits his surprise:

> Octopus is a colourful animal, capable of rapid colour change. It succeeds in matching its background and it

employs colour changes in a range of displays directed at its own kind and at other animals. *Prima facie,* one would expect octopuses to be able to distinguish between colours.[21]

When it is the octopus's turn to hunt rather than be hunted, it is a force to be reckoned with. The way in which an octopus finds food is what researchers have labelled 'speculative foraging'. That means octopuses go out looking for whatever comes their way, and some days, of course, it will take longer than others – not usually too long, though, because octopuses are not only fine hunters: they are also not too choosy. If it has meat and it's alive, an octopus will eat it. They locate prey by using one or more of three senses: sight, touch (with a long arm extended and searching for something to grab) and the equivalent of scent,

Up close and personal...

a chemical stimulation of receptor cells on the suckers of their arms. Experiments have shown that even when an octopus in a tank cannot see prey on the other side of a divider, it senses its presence there immediately.

When an octopus in the wild sights a potential meal, the idea is to get the prey under its mantle cavity as soon as possible, where it will be attacked by the beak and mouth. Sometimes it will pounce directly using what Hanlon called the 'parachute attack': descending on, enfolding and covering its victim. Henry Lee described the attack:

The eye of *Octopus vulgaris* is a sensitive instrument.

overleaf: (left) *O. vulgaris* on a reef.

(right) Giant Pacific octopus jets away.

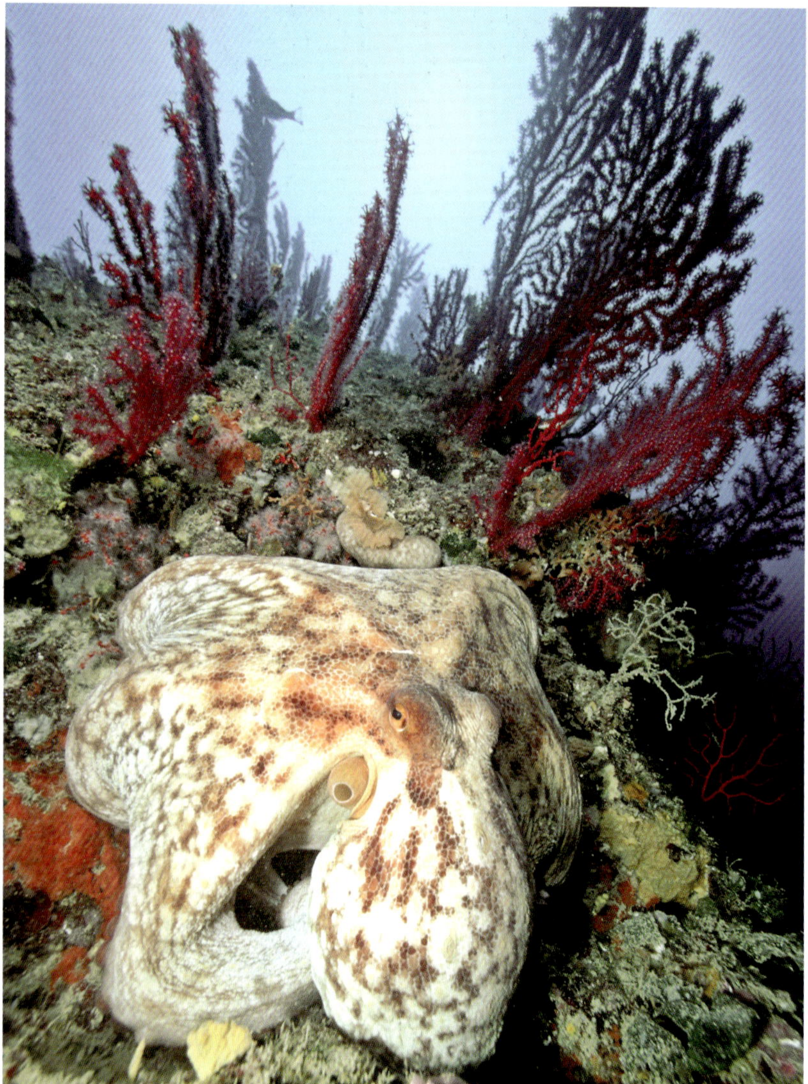

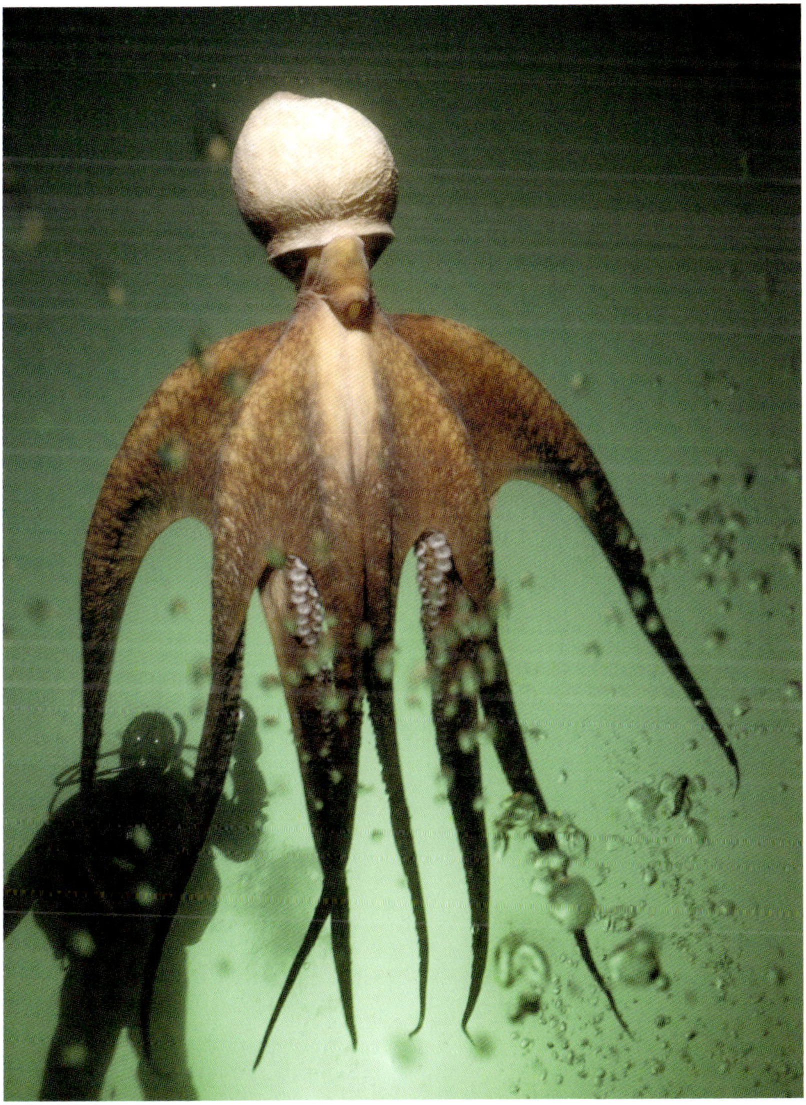

Octopus parachutes down on prey.

The action of an octopus when seizing its prey for its necessary food is very like that of a cat pouncing on a mouse, and holding it down beneath its paws. The movement is as sudden, the scuffle as brief, and the escape of the prisoner even less probable.[22]

At other times an octopus will lie on the bottom, looking for all the world like just another rock; suddenly an arm will whip out to capture a passing small fish or crab and stuff it under the mantle. Escape becomes highly unlikely once the prey is beneath that formidable web of flesh, being torn at by the beak and the tough, saw-toothed tongue called a radula, which is a powerful cross between a saw and a drill. At still other times, the octopus uses an arm to search for food in a narrow crack or crevice, often finding a crab or a shellfish that is holed up inside.

If the prey is a crab, one of the octopus's preferred meals, it may be opened with the hard, black, chitinous beak, aided by the radula, which the octopus keeps retracted until it is needed. In addition octopuses secrete a strong venom from their salivary glands which paralyses their prey and relaxes its musculature, rendering it helpless. The venom present in octopus saliva is currently being studied to discover which of its properties might be incorporated into medicines for human use.[23] Its effect on the crab is almost instantaneous, at which point the octopus uses its radula to finish opening the shell. Then it saws apart the paralysed muscle holding the crab's shell together. It scoops out every last morsel of meat, leaving behind an empty crab half-shell.

If it has captured a clam or a mussel, an octopus will use an array of tactics to extract meat from the shell: it may pull the clam

A painter walking along the seashore: Félix Buhot, *Le Peintre de marine*, 1872–91, drypoint and aquatint.

'Cephalopoda', from Richard Lydekker, *Royal Natural History*, vol. VI (1896).

apart using two of its strong arms, or drill a hole through the shell with beak and radula and inject venom, or perhaps carry out this same operation after chipping off an edge of the shell to expose the adductor muscle. In an article in *American Zoologist* in 1969, Jerome Wodinsky noted that common octopuses drilled into conch shells at the exact spot where the retractor muscle was attached, which the snail used to shrink into its shell. Wodinsky first covered this spot by taping on a piece of rubber that the octopus promptly tore off so it could drill. Then he applied a thin plastic covering and the octopus drilled through both plastic and shell at the same place. When he covered the spot with impenetrable metal, the octopus started drilling as close to the edge of the metal as was possible.[24]

Occasionally an octopus will snare a passing small fish to add to its dietary mix. Octopuses have small mouths, and it takes them a while to consume a fish, as they can only swallow small pieces of food. The oesophagus of an octopus is narrow, but octopus saliva is a strong digestive agent, breaking down flesh and making it easier to swallow. Overall digestion is a slow process for an octopus: it can take 36 hours for the remains of a crab to be excreted. So that it does not have to pass up a meal should one cross its path during that time, the octopus gut has a crop where food can be stored for later use.

Those who scuba dive in octopus territory know that the best way to see an octopus is to look for its den, instead of trying to find the animal itself. Rocks, along with empty crab and clam shells piled together, are easier to see than a camouflaged octopus. Once a den is found, the odds are not bad that an octopus will be at home, or, if not, that sooner or later one will be. Octopuses are both nocturnal and diurnal, active during parts of the day and parts of the night over the course of 24 hours, but they spend a lot of time at home, asleep or something very much like it, those big pop-eyes closed, their bodies at rest. When they capture food

Computer-generated graphic of an octopus walking underwater.

A veined octopus (*Amphioctopus marginatus*) appears to have made this beer bottle its home.

An octopus that has lost part of its arm.

they may bring it home to eat, depending on how far from their den the successful hunt takes place.

In 1991 Jennifer Mather, a professor of psychology and neuroscience from the University of Lethbridge in Alberta, Canada, spent her summer underwater off the coast of Bermuda, observing the daily lives of four juvenile *O. vulgaris*. She found that the animals spent 70 per cent of their time inside their dens. For the rest of the time, they were outside hunting. She observed that they had mini-cycles of hunting, eating and sleeping every six hours or so. What surprised her was finding that some 3 per cent of their days was spent in what she termed 'home maintenance'.[25] Octopuses regularly engage in house-cleaning: male or female, they will use their funnel to blow waste, empty shells and small rocks out of their dens until a midden forms outside.

In order to gain clues about the octopuses' eating habits, Mather used the same experimental method that some tabloid

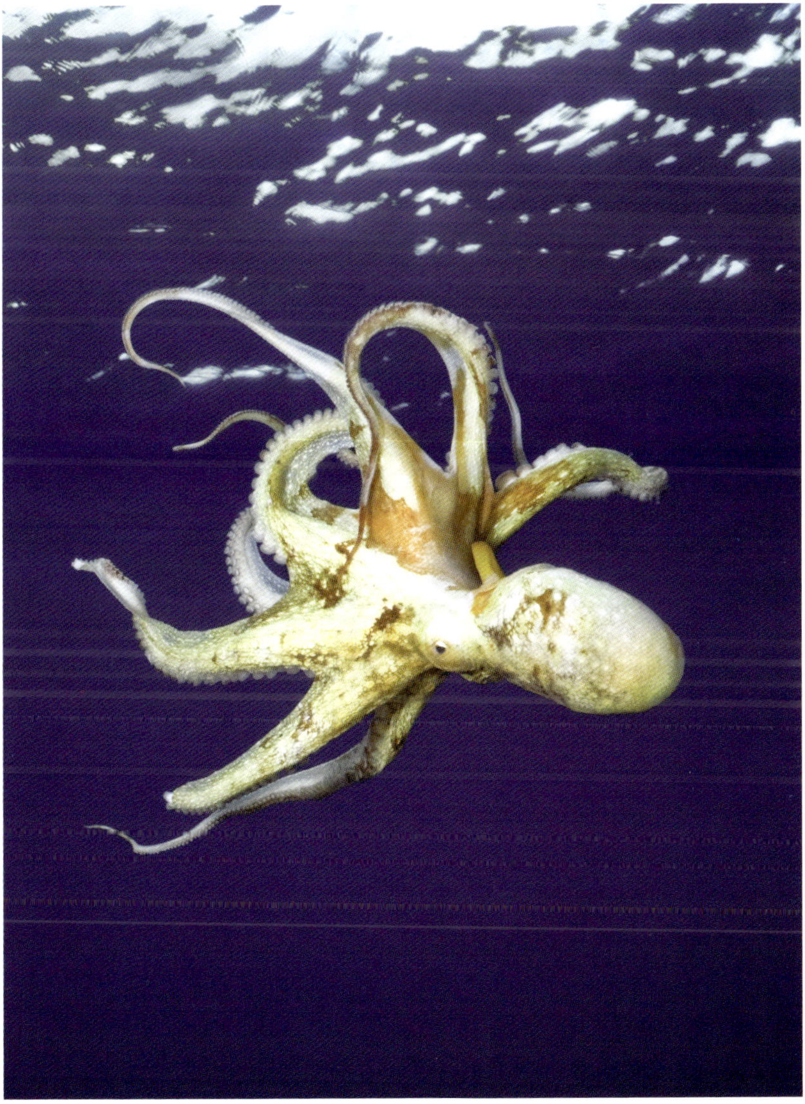

Clams are among the octopus's preferred foods.

newspaper writers use to dig into the lives of the rich and famous: she went through their garbage. What she found was that octopuses will eat almost any animal that can't get away from them. By examining an octopus's midden, its expelled pile of refuse, she found ample proof that they have catholic eating tastes. For instance, over four weeks, going through the trash of a dozen octopuses, she found 28 prey species, ranging from immature conch snails to shore crabs and shrimp.[26]

2 Octopus Brain

> The brain of the octopus has already abundantly proved
> its value for the study of behaviour. It is perhaps the type
> most divergent from that of mammals that is really suitable
> for study of the learning process.
> John Z. Young, *The Anatomy of the Nervous System of 'Octopus vulgaris'* (1971)

In his description of the octopus Aristotle made one glaring error, perhaps mistaking hunger, or curiosity, for stupidity. He observed that when a man's fingers were waggled in the water, an octopus would often charge them: 'The octopus is a stupid creature', he wrote, 'for it will approach a man's hand if it be lowered in the water.'[1] In fact, laboratory experiments have revealed that octopuses are far more intelligent than most marine creatures, and probably the most intelligent invertebrates in the world, but Aristotle's opinion held for a long time.

Scientists began studying the animal because it had a straightforward nervous system and a high pain threshold. It could stand all sorts of extirpations and amputations and still stay alive. Only in the second half of the twentieth century did scientists begin to examine the octopus's mind; before then it had not occurred to researchers that an octopus had much of a mental life. The octopus is, after all, an invertebrate, a marine mollusc distantly related to the clam. It belongs to the sub-class Coleoidea, along with the squid and the cuttlefish, and the class Cephalopoda, which includes the shell-less coleoids as well as the elegantly shelled nautiluses. None of these animals were thought have a lot of smarts.

The octopus is apparently a poor candidate for brain power. It has a lifespan of only a year or two and – to top it all off – is a solitary being, having little or no interaction with other members of its species. Why would such a creature need intelligence? What it needs are hunting skills, which the octopus has in abundance, and the defensive capacities that impressed Aristotle: it is able to assume the protective colouration of its surroundings in a wide range of subtle hues, and has the capability to spew out ink to distract a pursuer while it jets away. These are the things an octopus needs, and these are the things it has.

Yet an octopus's brain is larger and more complex even than those of many vertebrates like fish or reptiles, and much more so than those of most invertebrates. What's more, its brain shares features such as folded lobes and similar brainwave patterns with mammalian brains, although the octopus brain is wrapped around its oesophagus between the beak and the stomach, rather than resting in a cranium like that of humans. 'The [octopus] brain is anatomically complex', according to neuroscientist Ted Bullock of the University of California in San Diego. 'It is very highly differentiated. It has a lot of texture, it isn't smooth or monotonous. It looks like a complicated brain, histologically and microscopically.'[2]

Over virtually the entire twentieth century, the place where more information about the octopus brain was discovered than in any other was the Stazione Zoologica Anton Dohrn, a nineteenth-century building on the shore of the Bay of Naples which opened in 1873 as one of the world's first wholly dedicated marine research stations; it has been the site of many of the most important discoveries about octopus behaviour. The Stazione's founder, Anton Dohrn, was a biologist born in 1840 in Stettin, Pomerania, in what is now Poland. At the age of 33 he founded the Stazione. He was a strong supporter of Charles Darwin and corresponded with him regularly. Darwin, in turn, became an ardent and vocal fan of the Stazione and its young director, sending money when Dohrn's

The Naples Zoological Station c. 1875.

enterprise was financially pressed, and recommending it to British researchers. The results obtained in Naples contributed to confirming evolutionary theory, the nineteenth century's great scientific task.

Dohrn had begun work on the Stazione when he was only 29 years old, convincing officials in Naples to grant him land in the city's long, beautiful, public park by the bay, the Villa Comunale. The park is still a remarkable island of calm in what may be the most chaotic city in Europe. In Naples, with its ungoverned heavy foot and car traffic, crossing a street is an act of faith, but its noise and dust disappear in the 1-kilometre-long Villa Comunale park with its gazebos, royal palms, long promenade and benches in an orderly row. And right in the middle of that quiet space is the most historically important centre of octopus research in the world.

Dohrn's idea was that the Stazione would finance itself by renting well-equipped labs to researchers, as well as by building an aquarium on the ground floor to generate revenue through

Anton Dohrn, seated, with his wife Marie, c. 1905.

ticket sales to the public. He envisioned it as the first of a network of such research stations that he would establish around the world, places where scientists could come and collect specimens, make observations and do research, then pack up and move on to the next station. The Naples Stazione proved so time-consuming that he had his hands full just keeping it afloat, and all thoughts of establishing other stations quickly disappeared.[3]

The Stazione did not lack for researchers. A century ago Naples still had the elegance and glamour that had distinguished it for 300 years, its gardens, palaces and cathedrals drawing well-heeled visitors from all over Europe. It was a popular place to spend summers, or part of a university sabbatical, among people doing research work on marine animals. Twenty Nobel Prize-winners spent some time doing research at the Stazione in the twentieth century, and although Dohrn's plans for branch laboratories never materialized, the success of the Naples station inspired the building of other laboratories on the same principles, some of which are still functioning, including the Marine Biological Laboratory of the United Kingdom in Plymouth, Devon, which was founded in 1884, and the Woods Hole Oceanographic Institute in Woods Hole, Massachusetts, founded in 1930.

Early research at the Stazione focused on morphology, embryology and physiology. These were the fields on which the new science of zoology was concentrating in order to integrate itself into evolutionary theory. The Bay of Naples was rich in marine specimens, and from the Stazione's beginnings it was a particularly attractive place to work for researchers specializing in invertebrates and especially in octopuses. The original ironwork still on the gate at the entrance to the Stazione features crabs and octopuses.

The waters around Naples have traditionally teemed with *Octopus vulgaris*, and the animal features strongly in Neapolitan cuisine. Specimens abound, and the octopus has some advantages as a research species in addition to its learning capacity. It adapts quickly to captivity in only a few days, according to marine biologist Binyamin Hochner. 'This adaptation, or acclimatization, can easily be perceived by humans, as it involves a clear transition from a frightened, hiding octopus to a pet-like animal that behaves in a friendly way and attends to any event occurring in its aquarium area.'[4]

Various factors helped to shift the focus of scientific investigation from embryology and physiology to learning and behaviour.

One was the octopus's voracious appetite, which means that food will almost always work as a motivator. Octopuses also have natural curiosity and excellent eyesight; they rely on monocular vision, and individuals favour one eye over the other. Hochner points out that such lateralization, which corresponds to our right- and left-handedness, suggests specialization in the brain's hemispheres, once thought to be an exclusive trait of vertebrates. The other thing in its favour, he notes (although perhaps not from the animal's perspective), is that

> octopuses are resilient to invasive surgery and recover rapidly following lesions in their central nervous system under deep anaesthesia. Due to these advantages, the behaviour of *O. vulgaris* has been extensively studied, and its learning abilities have been characterized in captivity.[5]

Among the earliest research in learning done at the Stazione was a series of experiments by the German researcher Jakob von Uexküll in 1905. Uexküll was head of the physiology department at the Stazione for ten years, and carried out many experiments on the nervous and muscular systems of marine animals. He was also a pioneer of modern behavioural biology and the investigation of how living things connect to their environments.

In a groundbreaking experiment he starved some octopuses for fifteen days before releasing hermit crabs that were carrying sea anemones into the tanks. The famished octopuses rushed to devour this delicacy, but on being stung by the sea anemones they backed off, and subsequently refused to attack crabs carrying anemones, while they happily devoured crabs without them.[6]

The idea that octopuses could learn, that present events could influence their future behaviour, opened a whole new vista of octopus research early in the twentieth century as the animal's remarkable learning behaviours were observed. In 1910 a Frenchman from the Sorbonne, Henri Piéron, came to the Stazione. His experiments showed that when an octopus was presented with a jar that had a crab inside and was closed with a cork, the animal was capable of learning how to take out the cork. What's more, it remembered the lesson over time, getting quicker and quicker at reaching the crab.[7]

In work at the Stazione in 1932 the Dutch physiologist Frederik J. J. Buytendijk did training experiments with octopuses, reinforcing the idea that they could learn and remember, at least for a short time, what they learned. He used a 10-cm-square, white card attached to a stick. Initially, when he passed it near an octopus, the animal ducked its head, but after fifteen such movements with the card at one-second intervals, the octopus stopped reacting so brusquely, and merely watched the card attentively. If it saw the card again after five minutes, it ducked its head, but changed its behaviour after seeing the card only six times. If another five minutes was allowed to elapse, it would only take one movement of the card before the animal stopped ducking its head.[8]

One of the early ways to test octopus learning was through 'detour' trials. This work began at the Stazione with Paul Schiller in 1947. An octopus could see a crab through two chicken-wire windows with an opaque corridor between them. The octopus had to figure out how to use the corridor to reach the crab, and Schiller concluded that after a certain number of trials the octopus learned the correct route and repeated it consistently.[9]

An extraordinary number and range of experiments in octopus behaviour and neurophysiology were done at the Stazione in the 1950s and '60s by John Z. Young, a British neurophysiologist who died in 1997 at the age of 90. He first came to the Stazione in 1928 on a scholarship from Oxford University to study the

An octopus plays with a Rubik's cube.

Octopuses can learn how to open a jar that contains something good to eat.

autonomic nervous systems of fishes. In 1947 he began spending his summers at the Stazione, and continued to do so until 1975. Once established in 1947, he found funding for a research assistant and advertised the position. One of those who applied was a British PhD student, Brian B. Boycott, who later became a prominent neuroscientist in his own right. For Boycott, the position offered by Young was a dream come true. 'For a zoologist considering applying for Young's research assistantship, the romance and prestige of the Naples laboratory was as attractive as his very high and dynamic reputation', he wrote many years later.[10]

However, for the rather unworldly young Englishman, the experience provided much more than simply exciting lab work with octopuses. Boycott wrote of an evening in 1947 when he

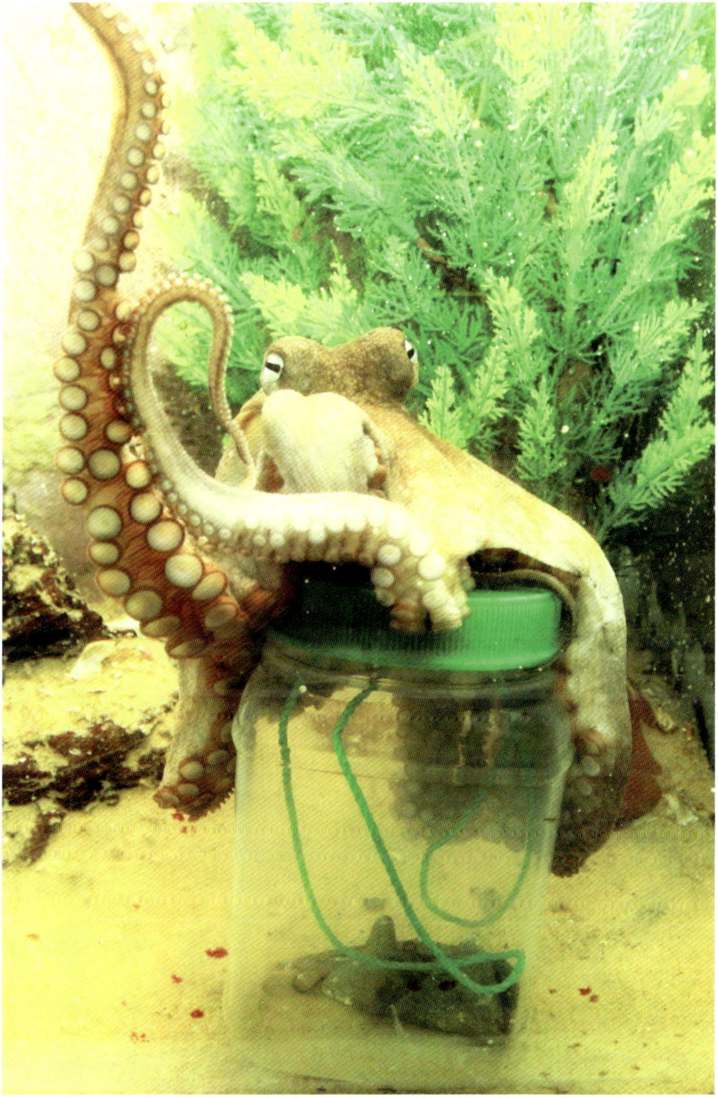

joined a group of Neapolitans gathered around a pre-war radio, set up on the sidewalk:

> It was tuned to catch the beginning of the first post-war production of a Verdi opera to be broadcast from La Scala. We were invited to sit with them. I cannot forget this. Nor, on another occasion, coming upon two small children who were begging passersby for money to bury their dead mother. She was lying on the street with the grandmother by her head. My learning curve during those early years in Naples was very steep. I could fill this whole article with such vivid reminisces, all influential to my development as a person. Indeed, I perhaps should list Naples and the Stazione under education rather than research.

The earliest work of Boycott and Young was to map cephalopod brains by contrasting the structural organization of the motor control systems with their memory systems, what Boycott called 'a time-honoured comparative anatomical approach in a search for the basic features of an organ system'. For this they used 'electrical stimulation and surgical ablation of the brains'.[11] What this boiled down to was training an octopus, then cutting out specific parts of its brain to see which were required for memory of a lesson previously learned. Boycott's first task was to develop a training system, and he eventually opted for presenting a visual discrimination between crabs alone, which are a tasty meal to the octopus, and crabs presented with a small white square, which delivered a low electric shock if the octopus attacked. 'Thus an octopus with the vertical and/or superior frontal lobes removed could not remember that an attack on a crab presented with a white plate resulted in a nociceptive stimulus', wrote Boycott – a polite way of saying, *it hurt*. Animals with intact brains quickly learned and remembered not to attack the crab with the white square. Alternatively a reward system could be used: if an octopus attacks a crab with a small white square, it is immediately rewarded with food. Experiments proved that the attacks came more rapidly the more times they were rewarded. 'Repeated presentations and feedings lead to increasingly vigorous attacks, so that after a few trials, the typical approach is a jet-propelled leap from the home onto the target as soon as this is lowered into the water.'[12]

Based on many such experiments, Young deduced that the octopus brain had separate centres for visual and tactile memory, with some slight overlap. From 1955 to 1965 his work at the Stazione was largely concentrated on the octopus's capacity for visual discrimination between figures showed at one end of a tank. As with the memory system experiments, either a reward or a punishment was used to reinforce behaviour. Then, in the mid-1960s, he began to look closely at the work on tactile discrimination being done at the Stazione by another outstanding British researcher, Martin J. Wells, who taught zoology at Cambridge University.

Wells's career was also inextricably bound up with the Stazione. His first stay was in 1953. He was beginning the research that would result in his seminal volume, *Octopus: Physiology and Behaviour of an Advanced Invertebrate* (1978). In an interview of 8 December 1998 with the *New York Times*, which called him 'one of the world's great experts on cephalopods', Wells recalled that in his early years at the Stazione, studying octopus and squid, he frequently ate his research subjects. 'Oh', he told the interviewer, 'when my wife and I were first married, I had a job on the staff of Naples Zoological Station in Italy, and we were very impoverished. So of course, we ate our experimental animals. The only thing we had to do for the laboratory was save their brains. We ate calamari till we got pig-sick of it.'

Much of Wells's early work dealt with the capacity of octopuses to learn by using touch. He trained them to discriminate by touch between bivalves of different species and objects with different surfaces, such as grooved or smooth, and showed they could remember what they had learned.[13] As Young studied the work Wells was doing, he wondered where the tactile memories would be stored. Young took octopuses and trained them using plastic balls – some with three stripes cut into them and some with nine. When they chose the ball with three, they were rewarded, and with nine they were shocked. They learned quickly. Then he began to lesion their brains. 'After a few trials, one ball was quickly taken under the web, and the other ball ejected', he wrote. 'To avoid visual choice, the optic nerves were first cut, but in fact the octopus cannot make the distinction visually, and reliable results were obtained with intact animals.'

It was not vision the animals were using to discriminate, but tactile information that was being processed by the octopus. Young's schematic of the octopus brain consisted of two lobes surrounding the animal's oesophagus – the supraoesophageal mass and the suboesophageal mass – and he found that tactile discrimination was not only being processed in the supraoesophageal mass, but that the tactile memory was distributed between different parts of the lobe.

> After splitting the whole of the supraoesophageal lobe, we found that the two sides can be trained independently, even performing in opposite directions. Thus, it is possible to compare the effects of different lesions in the same animal ... We found that removing each of the lobes reduced learning to a different extent. The tactile memory is therefore distributed between them, as is the visual memory ...

This was a long series of experiments spread over several years in Naples.[14]

Both separately and together, Wells and Young did groundbreaking cephalopod research at the Stazione. In 1971 Young published *The Anatomy of the Nervous System of 'Octopus vulgaris'*, the fruit of more than 40 years of research, much of it at the Stazione. In 1991, more than 60 years after his first visit, Naples honoured him with a key to the city. In an autobiographical essay published in 2001, at the age of 88, he looked back on his career and concluded, 'I have advanced knowledge of the operation of cephalopod brains and so helped toward the understanding of brains in general.'[15]

Octopus catching a lobster, illustration from an edition of *Die Gartenlaube*, 1894.

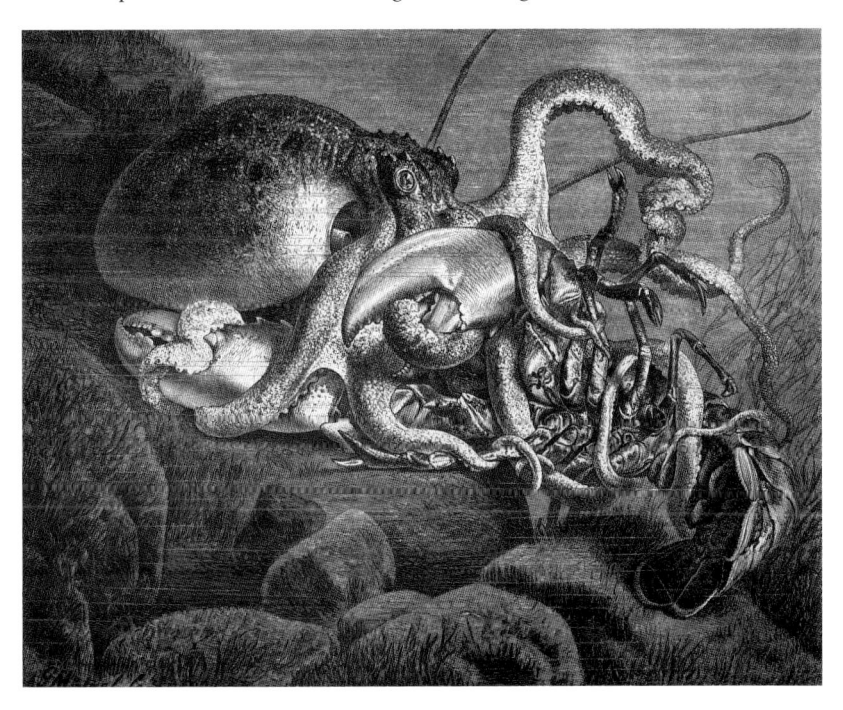

Even as Martin Wells and John Young mapped the octopus brain and neural networks with ever-increasing precision, the Stazione was undergoing financial difficulties and administrative battles. Dohrn himself had died in 1909, and while his descendants took an active interest in the Stazione, its management passed through several administrations, some of which were more capable than others. By the mid-1970s the Stazione had gone through some hard times with thin financial resources and internal management problems. In 1986 it was finally fully funded as a national research institute, and continues to serve as an investigative facility, although is no longer a private one. The system of renting lab space has been eliminated, and the 37 research groups that were installed there in 2011 each had its own funding. The small aquarium on the first floor is still open to the public, and is a popular destination for schoolfield trips.[16]

The octopus behaviour experiments done at the Stazione drew attention from cephalopod researchers around the world. By the early 1960s, as the experiments piled up, it became clear that octopuses had a sophisticated learning capacity. Between 1959 and 1980 some 200 papers were published on different aspects of the learning process of the common octopus, and the more research data that piled up, the more impressive the octopus brain appeared.

For instance, in another trait they shared with many vertebrates, octopuses rapidly learned to press a lever if food was delivered when they did so. The first to show this, in 1959, was Peter B. Dews, a professor at the Harvard School of Pharmacology. Dews worked closely with a Harvard colleague, the legendary behaviourist B. F. Skinner, and was one of the early researchers to test the behavioural effects of drugs like methamphetamine and phenobarbital on animals, mostly pigeons. His earliest research, in 1945, was on the effects of tetrahydracannabinol, the psychoactive ingredient in marijuana.

Dews's work set the foundation for much of today's pharmacological approach to mental illness. An article about him in the *Journal of the Experimental Analysis of Behaviour* said,

> The experimental findings generated by Dews' research, blending the sophisticated use of behaviour and pharmacological principles together with the elegant manner of their presentation and far-reaching implications, provided the force and momentum to establish and direct behavioural pharmacology for several decades.[17]

Although it was in pharmacology that he gained the most renown, the octopuses were spared that side of Dews's research. His experiments with *O. vulgaris* grew out of his curiosity about the degree to which invertebrates were capable of operant behaviour, modifying their behaviour in reaction to previous consequences, a behavioural theory first posited by Skinner. 'If the phenomena of operant behaviour are to be found in the octopus as well as in the vertebrate species studied, then these phenomena probably are of very general biological significance', wrote Dews.[18]

He used a trio of octopuses that he named Albert, Bertram and Charles. Two of the three, Albert and Bertram, proved to be quick learners and cooperative, particularly after having not been fed for 24 hours. Once they learned that pressing a lever would deliver food, they willingly continued to press the lever for twelve days before the lesson learned started to fade. However Dews admitted later that the third octopus had proved to be a startlingly different story.

Whereas Albert and Bertram gently operated the lever while free-floating, Charles anchored several tentacles on the side of the tank and others around the lever and applied great force. The lever was bent a number of times, and on the 11th day was broken, leading to a premature termination of the experiment.

In addition Charles repeatedly reached out of the water with a long arm and pulled down a lamp suspended above the tank. He also directed jets of water at any human who got within range of his tank, something that Albert and Bertram never did. An octopus can expel large quantities of water from a muscular funnel just above its mantle, and, in fact, in its respiratory process it draws in water through a pair of valves and expels it through the funnel. Charles pointed his funnel and soaked anyone who came within range, clearly making known his feelings towards his keepers.

'The animal spent much time with eyes above the surface of the water, directing a jet of water at any individual who approached the tank', wrote Dews. 'This behaviour interfered materially with the smooth conduct of the experiments, and is, again, clearly incompatible with lever-pulling.'[19]

This kind of behaviour seemed to indicate not only that octopuses were quick learners, but that they had distinct personalities and ways of approaching their environment. At the end of the twentieth century researchers were once again rethinking their assumptions about octopus intelligence. Over the course of the century, the octopus brain had been revealed as complex and interesting, far beyond what nineteenth-century marine investigators had imagined. As the twenty-first century approached some octopus researchers wanted to go much further. They ascribed more advanced behaviours like observational learning and play to octopuses, and designed experiments to show that the animals have a variety of individual personalities. These scientists generally subscribed to a theory that octopuses have 'simple consciousness' and 'self-awareness' – that they have a mind as well as a brain.[20]

3 Octopus Mind

> The difficulties of imagining an intelligent mollusc are embodied in octopus websites, many of which alternate stories of octopus intelligence with recipes for cooking the animal.
> Eugene Linden, *The Octopus and the Orangutan* (2003)

Even given the octopus's remarkable learning ability, it was hard for many researchers to conceive that the folds of its brain harboured real intelligence. Yet if you look an octopus in the eye you can see intelligence in the octopus's gaze. This intelligence is demonstrable in the laboratory. The generally accepted conclusion today is that an octopus has more or less the same level of intelligence as a dog or a cat, and most researchers who work with octopuses agree that the creatures have personalities and markedly different individual temperaments.

In 1992 the world of octopus research was shaken to the core when *Science* published an article by an Italian neurobiologist, Graziano Fiorito, who – no surprise – was working at the Stazione Zoologica Anton Dohrn. He had designed an experiment that concluded octopuses were more clever than anyone had previously imagined, and claimed to have proven that they were capable of observational learning. This means that they could learn something new simply by watching it done by another octopus: a level of intelligence never before ascribed to an invertebrate.

The ability to translate observation into learning and action requires a capacity to 'integrate information to produce adaptive behavioural patterns', as Fiorito wrote in his *Science* article.[1] Observational learning meant using a sophisticated mental process beyond anything previously attributed to a cephalopod. If an invertebrate such as an octopus and a vertebrate like a primate develop similar mental capacities for the organization of information, understanding the biology of how this is done could reveal a basic functional principle of evolution shared by vertebrate and invertebrate alike.

Born and raised in Naples, Graziano Fiorito turned down a chance to join E. O. Wilson's group at Harvard in the mid-1980s in order to accept an offer from the Stazione in his home town. His original interest when he came to the Stazione was crabs. In 1985 Fiorito saw a picture in a Jacques Cousteau book showing an octopus opening a jar to prey on a crab. These days, videos of an octopus doing just that are widely available on the Internet, but in those days it caught Fiorito's attention.

'This was tremendously interesting', said Fiorito, a short, clean-shaven, slightly stooped man with thinning brown hair and lively brown eyes.

> I went to the literature and found for sure that octopus could solve such a problem. It's important, because this kind of problem-solving in terms of behaviour is highly complex and demonstrates impressive cognitive capabilities. In 1986, I finished my last experiment with crabs, and thereafter I have dedicated all my life to octopus.[2]

The methodology of Fiorito's experiment was simple: first, an octopus in a tank was presented with two balls, a red ball and a white one. The red one had a fish attached, positioned in such a way that the octopus could not see it. Those that chose the red ball could eat the fish. The white ball had no fish and, in addition, brought a dose of pain: an electric shock for those animals that chose it. It took an octopus an average of sixteen trials, each

Australian watercolour of an octopus, late 18th century, artist unknown.

consisting of five attempts, before it chose the red ball without error, *always*, and continued to do so even after the reward was discontinued. For a second group the balls were reversed – white brought pleasure, red brought pain – and it took these octopuses an average of 21.5 trials before they learned always to choose the white ball.

Fiorito called these trained octopuses 'demonstrators'. Next door to them, in the same tank but separated by a transparent wall, an 'observer' octopus was housed. The observers were given the opportunity to watch four successful trials with the demonstrators. While the tests were under way the observers usually interrupted whatever they were doing to watch the goings-on next door. 'From the analysis of video recordings we noted that observer octopuses increased their attention during each of the trials', wrote Fiorito. 'In particular, we noted that the observers followed the action patterns of their demonstrators with movements of their head and eyes.'[3]

After this the observer octopuses were placed in the tank with the balls. No rewards or shocks were given to the observers, so this could not be posited as an explanation for the amazing thing that happened. The observer octopuses that had watched the demonstrators attack the red ball did the same thing a significantly higher number of times than they attacked the white. In fact, Fiorito's article reported, out of 150 trials with these observers, they chose to attack the red ball 129 times, the white one thirteen times, and neither eight times. The error rate was higher among observers that had watched demonstrators with white balls, but still, out of 70 trials, the white ball was chosen 49 times and the red only seven. They ran the trials again five days later, and the results were basically the same. Fiorito concluded that the experiment was clear evidence that observational learning could occur in octopuses.

Many of his colleagues were not so sure. The idea that an octopus was capable of observational learning was greeted with surprise and scepticism in some camps. Why would an animal with a solitary and self-sufficient life need observational learning? Some scientists sharply criticized aspects of the experiment's methodology, including an absence of adequate control experiments.[4] Concern was also voiced that the researchers were visible to the observer octopuses during the trials, and could inadvertently have given visual cues to the animals.

Fiorito understands the sceptical reception his work received from some of his colleagues, but says that they're wrong. 'Yes, they are solitary animals, but that does not mean they're asocial', Fiorito told me in 2010. 'It means solitary. So my idea was to look and see if the animal that *can* do could convey any kind of information to the animal that *can't* do in order to facilitate its learning capability.'[5]

It was not the first time that research on octopus learning at the venerable Stazione had been challenged. In 1963, for instance, Peter Dilly, an anatomist from University College London, spent his summer at the Stazione carrying out an experiment that seemed to demonstrate that octopuses retained what they observed, at least for a while. An individual *Octopus vulgaris* in a tank was shown two identical white plastic rectangles for 30 seconds. Next to one of the rectangles was a crab. They were side by side but divided by a partition at the opposite end from the octopus and its home. A transparent wall kept the octopus from attacking the crab. The transparent wall was covered for ten seconds while the crab was removed; then the wall itself was removed. In 21 out of 24 trials, the octopus immediately attacked the rectangle where the crab had been. 'It is clear that an octopus can choose the correct response', wrote Dilly in the *Journal of Experimental Biology*, 'even after the object stimulating that response has been removed from the visual field.'[6]

Jeff Bitterman, criticizing Dilly's experiment in *Invertebrate Learning* (1975), remembered his own visit to an octopus research lab at the Stazione, and deplored the conditions in which the octopuses were kept, as well as a lack of scientific rigour in Dilly's experiments. In addition he questioned whether coming to the Stazione for the summer to do experiments might not encourage sloppy technique. He wrote that a scientist working there told him that he 'only had a short time to spend there each year and that time devoted to improving the technique would yield no data.'[7]

But Graziano Fiorito was no summer visitor. He would still be at the Stazione twenty years after his startling claims for observational learning, still doing groundbreaking investigation of learning and memory in octopuses, and still defending his 1992 experiment. When I visited the 53-year-old neurobiologist in 2010 he had just completed a series of experiments demonstrating that an octopus was not only capable of learning by watching another octopus, but could even learn by watching a videotape.

By his own account, Fiorito was stung by the criticism that had greeted his article of 1992, but not deterred. 'I decided to respond to the critics with silence and continued research, and that's what I have done', he told me. 'The fact is that octopus brains may have computational complexity and perception capabilities that allow them to understand what is happening in their surroundings. What we want to see is if a simple animal may have the neural basis of cognition and consciousness.'

No other researchers have successfully repeated Fiorito's experiments of 1992, but after his article appeared in *Science*, a new awareness grew among scientists that octopuses possessed some remarkable behavioural qualities, which could include some level of intelligence. Fiorito's experiment opened up a way for researchers to begin to think in different ways about the octopus, and to expand the kinds of hypotheses traditionally posed by scientists investigating these invertebrates.

Researchers like Jennifer Mather and Roland Anderson were able to take seriously the hypothesis that every octopus has a personality. In 1993 Anderson, the director of the Seattle Aquarium, teamed up with Mather, a professor of psychology and neuroscience from the University of Lethbridge in Alberta, Canada. Anderson spent 31 years at the Seattle Aquarium before retiring in 2009. The son of a sea captain, he grew up near the ocean and became an avid scuba diver. Over the course of his tenure at the aquarium, he became fascinated by the natural history, behaviour and aquarium husbandry of marine invertebrates, especially the cold-water cephalopods of Puget Sound.[8]

Mather's voice rings with enthusiasm when she talks about octopuses. She has been researching them since the mid-1970s.

There are four species of deadly blue-ringed octopuses from the genus *Hapalochlaena*.

She was raised in Victoria, on the coast of British Columbia, and was fascinated early on by marine life. Now she finds herself studying it as a tenured professor in landlocked Lethbridge. It is an academic town that rears up out of the plains and the wheat fields, a long way from the closest salt water. However, Mather is not an academic, lab-bound researcher who has never done the dance down in the deep with her subjects. She spends her summers underwater in Bermuda, the Caribbean or Hawaii. Much of her early academic work was based on observation in the wild. 'I'm a real fanatic about fieldwork', she told an interviewer. 'I think that out there where they live is where you should be studying them.'[9]

Both Mather and Anderson had previously observed octopuses that appeared to have different personalities. Mather had found while watching common octopuses (*O. vulgaris*) underwater in the Caribbean that some were 'approachable', while others were not so; and in the laboratory, those she defined as 'emotional' could never achieve spatial learning, while others of a steadier nature were able to do consistently well in maze experiments by using landmarks for orientation. Anderson, working at the aquarium with Puget Sound's giant Pacific octopus (*Octopus dofleini*), as well as the diminutive *Enteroctopus rubescens*, had encountered animals with personality types that he described as including 'aggressive, indifferent, and paranoid'.

He was particularly impressed when, coming to work one morning, he found that one of the giant Pacific octopuses he was keeping in a tank had dug up the gravel on the tank's bottom, bitten through the cables attaching the under-gravel filter to the tank, and ripped apart the filter itself. The aquarium's staff had

Octopus colours.

already dubbed the animal Lucretia McEvil due to her generally mean and ill-tempered ways, and Anderson later wrote that it appeared she had worked out in advance just what to do. 'It looked like a careful sequencing/planning of actions and learning put to use, though the reasons weren't at all obvious.'[10]

They designed an experiment to identify distinct personality traits in octopuses using *O. rubescens*, a small reddish animal commonly found in the Puget Sound area around Seattle. They tested a total of 44 octopuses. Each octopus was put in its own tank with an artificial black Plexiglas den waiting for it. Testing began on the second day after capture and lasted for two weeks, with twelve hours of light and twelve of darkness daily. The researchers looked for individual differences of behaviour in three types of situation: alert, under threat and feeding. In the alert category, the lid of the tank was opened and the observer's head brought close to the opening at the front and centre of the octopus's sightline. Faced with the observer, the 44 subjects showed seven different responses, which included changing skin colour, bobbing their heads and shrinking back. When threatened, which was accomplished by putting a small wire brush in the tank and slowly approaching the octopus with it until contact was made, behaviours ranged from an ink blast, to crawling away, to aggressively grasping the brush. In the feeding category they noted that when a crab was introduced into the tank, some individuals would jet through the water to capture it, while others would walk along the bottom to get it, and still others would wait until the crab wandered within grabbing distance.

Mather and Anderson elaborated three forms of behaviour in which octopuses differed, which they call activity, reactivity, and avoidance. With these three they could take any individual octopus and create a 'personality profile'. When they analysed their results Mather and Anderson concluded that octopuses did have consistent individual differences in their behaviour in given situations. They reported their findings in the *Journal of Comparative Psychology* in 1993:

> Does this mean that octopuses have personalities and that these individual differences have a major effect on their learning and adaptation? The answer to the first question may be a qualified yes. These are more than situation-specific individual differences. They were long-lasting in observation and testing . . . and present in several situations.[11]

This was the first research that Jennifer Mather and Roland Anderson worked on together, but not the last. They proved to be a good scientific match because they were both open to thinking about octopus consciousness in wider terms than simply neurological systems or standard learning exercises. Anderson had Puget Sound's octopuses at his disposal, not only the small *O. rubescens*, but also the giant *O. dolfleini*, the largest of the world's known 300 or so species of octopus. Mather brought her behavioural and biological expertise.

In 1998 Mather and Anderson designed an experiment to determine whether octopuses were capable of play. They tested eight giant Pacific octopuses by putting an empty pill bottle in a tank with a slow water current that would carry the floating plastic bottle towards the octopus. Two of them showed signs of what might have been play when they waited for the bottle to come close, then jetted water at it until it reached the far end of the tank, and waited until it floated to them again before jetting more water and sending it to the other end again. The two octopuses both repeated this action more than twenty times, Mather and Anderson reported in the *Journal of Comparative Psychology*.[12]

The experiment with play may sound frivolous, but the ability to play, and to derive satisfaction from time spent doing so, was previously assumed to be the exclusive province of vertebrates, much as observational learning had been. This experiment, like Fiorito's in 1992, drew its share of detractors. However, Mather insists:

> Octopuses play – this is something it was presumed that only highly intelligent animals do. We never thought invertebrates did it. Play, obviously, is the exertion of intelligence, exploring the environment, gaining information from the environment, figuring out what to do about the environment. Finding that really was quite exciting.[13]

Jennifer Mather does not seem to mind when she is criticized for pushing the limits of people's notions about octopuses. In fact, she seems to encourage it. An article she wrote for the *American Malacological Bulletin* in 2008 was titled, 'To Boldly Go Where No Mollusc Has Gone Before: Personality, Play, Thinking, and Consciousness in Cephalopods'. The cephalopod she has in mind is the octopus, and she posits that it has what she calls a 'simple consciousness' and self-awareness. She writes, 'Such primary consciousness would be the result of an emergent central representation of the world and oneself.'[14]

The study of octopus learning and behaviour is by no means an overcrowded field of marine biology, and a lot remains to be discovered. Mather's take is that researchers should think big. She represents the branch of octopus investigation that is open to departing from traditional invertebrate studies, and includes the possibility that not only does octopus intelligence exist, but that it may encompass capacities and feelings to which we can easily relate and which have not previously been ascribed to any invertebrate. Mather feels that her dual qualifications as both a biologist and a behavioural psychologist have given her the tools to do just that.

> The biological background has brought me the understanding of the animal and the ecosystem, and the behaviour and the psychological approach has brought me the tools to ask specific questions. I can take the psychological questions and bring them to an animal that usually only biologists think about.[15]

A more standard approach to octopus intelligence research is represented by Jean Boal at Millersville University in Pennsylvania. Boal was a graduate student in ecology at the University of North Carolina in 1992, specializing in cephalopods, and an early supporter of Fiorito and Scotto when they published their results about observational learning. Her initial reaction was positive, as quoted in a *Science News* article which was picked up by the wire services and ran widely the day after Fiorito and Scotto's article came out. She speculated that perhaps octopuses had developed observational learning to ensure their survival in the wild. An octopus has no relationship with either parent after it hatches, so the young animal must learn to forage and avoid predators by watching other octopuses. 'Many people have considered observational learning to be a social skill that you would not expect in solitary animals', she said in her initial assessment of Fiorito's work. 'Yet octopuses can do it.'[16]

Later, after Boal was unable to replicate the experiment, she began to have her doubts, coming to believe that an octopus probably does not need observational learning to get along. Eventually she became overtly sceptical of the Naples results. 'As I added more controls, I got less and less evidence for learning', she told Garry Hamilton in an interview in 1997. 'I found there were a lot of places where people could have provided inadvertent cues to their performance.'[17]

By 1997 Boal had finished her PhD and joined the faculty at Millersville University as a professor of animal behaviour and marine biology. She decided to concentrate on the kinds of learning that octopuses *would* require in their lives and began to study the ways in which spatial learning is important to them. What she concluded was that octopuses employ a type of learning called conditional discrimination in which animals must discriminate between visual cues using an awareness of where they are and what they need to do, another type of learning generally associated with vertebrates.

Boal discovered that octopuses could learn how to find their way through a maze, discriminating between two burrows when one only looked like a burrow but was closed, blocking off access to the bait crab. They learned how to consistently choose the route to the open one.[18] This ability to learn spatially using visual cues was also observed in the wild by Jennifer Mather in 1991. She observed octopuses off the coast of Bermuda that were able to range as far away from their dens as 55 m (180 ft), and could still find their way back home using a different route from the one they took when they left.[19]

Why should an octopus have developed an intelligence and a capacity for learning? One possible reason is that it is descended from animals that had shells, without which octopuses are vulnerable. When cephalopods had shells, their strategy for staying alive was defensive, since they were well protected. Without shells they had to develop new strategies for survival. They had to improve their sensory and nervous systems and to rely more heavily on their vision, and they developed a larger brain with a capacity to learn.

An octopus is not the only creature that has evolved an intelligence in response to the vulnerability of being naked. Human beings might be said to have followed the same path. Perhaps this is an example of evolutionary convergence between ourselves and octopuses, although more research is needed to establish it. Jennifer Mather wrote in 2002:

> Similarities that could lead us to understand the evolution of intelligence in octopuses and humans are few, but thought-provoking: 1) neither group has the protection of exoskeleton, scales or armour, 2) both have evolved in complex environments, the octopod in the tropical coral reef and the hominid in the savannah edge, and 3) both have considerable variability among individuals and the ability of being able to change their behaviour to help them survive. So, perhaps looking at the octopuses through their intelligence, feeding flexibility, predator avoidance, play, and personality, helps us also look at aspects of ourselves, from another angle![20]

If an octopus's intelligence is an evolutionary response to some condition in its life as a cephalopod, then could a similar intelligence be found in the octopus's relatives, the squid and the cuttlefish? Good question, thought Jean Boal, who started doing research with cuttlefish in 1993. She has concluded that they have some remarkable qualities. One thing she has shown, by running cuttlefish through mazes, is that they have much the same ability to learn spatially as octopuses. In an interview with the PBS television programme *Nova* in 2005 she had high praise for them:

> Cuttlefish have the most splendid body patterns – they're just mesmerizing. Most people, when they see the way

the cuttlefish can change their body patterns, they're totally captivated. On top of that they have all kinds of cool social behaviour that octopuses just don't have. I think once you see the body patterning and the social interactions in cuttlefish, you're captivated for life. They're really splendid.

They don't have that immediate kind of grab-at-you personality at first that an octopus does. But if you ever look at one eye-level, I think you get pretty caught up in cuttlefish, too. Based on my experience, I couldn't rank cuttlefish and octopuses, for example, with one being smarter than the other. I think one might be better at one task than the other, because of the way they learn, and by the way the experiment is designed.[21]

Jean Boal and Jennifer Mather have distinctly different approaches to their cephalopod research, and each has her own vision of what the future of octopus investigation may hold. What they share is a basic respect for the animals' capacities, and both agree that what were accepted for many years as the limitations of invertebrate behaviour and biology need to be rethought in the light of ongoing cephalopod research.

Many octopuses have had their brains mapped, much of their neurological pathways have been diagrammed and experimentally severed, and a great deal of octopus behaviour has been studied. For all that laboratory work – all the slicing and dicing, observing and dissecting – a clear picture of how their minds function, or if they can be said to have minds at all, has yet to emerge. Whether what is at work is a sophisticated intelligence or something else entirely remains, for the moment, unresolved.

In 2011 Graziano Fiorito was still at it, working with the Israeli neurobiologist Binyamin Hochner, doing research that is very much in line with Mather's idea that to look at octopuses helps us to understand ourselves. Hochner described the work he was doing in collaboration with the Stazione and Fiorito:

> Nature has provided several examples of convergent evolutionary processes where similar functions are mediated by analogous systems in evolutionary [sic] remote species. This evolution of analogous systems, believed to be driven by the same selection forces, results in independent arrival at the most optimal solution for a particular task. Use of a comparative approach to study an invertebrate with vertebrate-like behaviour may therefore advance our analysis of brain mechanisms that are important for mediation of complex behaviours and learning and memory. The octopus is an ideal animal for such a study, as it is a unique invertebrate mollusc with learning abilities similar to those of vertebrates.[22]

Octopus behaviour has a level of sophistication unequalled in any other invertebrate. Researchers hope that by identifying and studying the mechanisms they have evolved for dealing with their world, clues may be uncovered that will help us understand our own evolution and development as cognitive beings.

4 Octopus Fishing, Farming and Marketing

An octopus pot –
inside, a short-lived dream
under the summer moon
Matsuo Bashō (1644–1694)

The genius of a great octopus broker is being able to judge supply and demand so well that the amount of animals purchased, and in storage awaiting shipping, stays low and constant. That's the way to make money in the octopus business, say those in the know. Enough product always has to be on hand to satisfy clients who demand it, and fishing boats that bring octopus to sell are counting on a plant to buy it, or they'll go elsewhere. At the same time, keeping a lot of octopuses on hand will only create a glut on the market, depress prices and run up storage bills.

Octopuses are bought and sold in many places around the world, but the most important is in the Canary Islands where it is processed, frozen and shipped to various parts of the globe. A substantial market for the fresh product also exists in Japan, where octopus is processed into sushi and sold in the United States or on the national Japanese market, and in a number of Mediterranean ports where it goes into the local market. World capture in 2007 was about 38,000 tonnes, according to the Food and Agriculture Organization of the United Nations (FAO).[1] Currently the octopus population in the Atlantic is stable, so far as researchers can tell, although not in optimum health.[2]

The plants in the Canary Islands are built to handle industrial trawlers. Each plant has factory ships under contract that are out at sea, dragging the bed for octopus with otter trawls,

Red octopus on coral reef.

pulverizing anything delicate in their paths and virtually vacuuming up *Octopus vulgaris*. This kind of fishing can rapidly deplete a resource, and it is no surprise that the factory ships have moved steadily south over the past fifteen years, from the Atlantic Ocean off Spain and Portugal down to Morocco and Mauritania. In 1997 the catch of octopus from Spanish and Portuguese waters was about 44 tonnes, but by 2003 that was down to 27.5 tonnes.[3]

Even though the numbers of captured octopuses are down in Spain and Portugal, they still vary substantially from year to year depending on wind and weather, making it difficult to make a reliable stock assessment. Other problems hamper arriving at accurate conclusions about the health and size of octopus populations: data collection methods are not what they might be, spawning goes on all year, and so does fishing in many places, all of which contributes to making it extremely difficult to model the *O. vulgaris* population and determine what, if any, controls should be imposed on its capture.

In addition the prospect of climate change and altered environmental conditions present a set of unknowns about the immediate future. Both global warming and ocean acidification could diminish the world's octopus population, say researchers, because of the ways in which they might affect egg development and other aspects of octopus life. Currently the world octopus population is still abundant enough to support numerous fisheries around the world. The largest is off the North African coast based in a small city, Dakhla, in the Western Sahara between Morocco and Mauritania, where the desert runs into the Atlantic Ocean, 240 km (150 miles) north of the Mauritanian border.

This small, urban centre surrounded by desert has a population of some 70,000 people, and is one of the oldest settlements in the Western Sahara. It was founded by the Spanish in 1502 under the name Villa Cisneros. During the colonial period in the late nineteenth century, Spain named Villa Cisneros the capital of the province of Río de Oro (Gold River), one of the two regions of the Spanish Sahara. A prison camp existed there during the Spanish Civil War. For much of the twentieth century, however, it was a sleepy port with a jumble of narrow streets, a small outpost of Spanish soldiers, some relics of colonial architecture and a crumbling cathedral. In 1975, shortly before he died, the Spanish dictator Francisco Franco renounced all territorial rights to the Western Sahara in the name of Spain, and withdrew all Spanish troops.

Now, thanks chiefly to octopus, Moroccan-administered Dakhla is a gold-rush town, and following the completion of new facilities in 2005, it is Morocco's largest fishing port (although whether it rightly belongs to Morocco depends on who you ask). Dakhla has more than 90 octopus processing plants,[4] and its production lines are often overseen by representatives of Japanese seafood companies, making sure that what is culled for export to Japan is of high quality.

The offshore Atlantic from Senegal north to Mauritania and Morocco is part of the Northwest Africa upwelling system, an oceanic region favoured by the common octopus. The waters off the coast of Dakhla are among the most productive octopus fishing grounds in the world, but the numbers have declined in the past few years due to intensive fishing by factory ships from Spain, Portugal, China and Japan.

Dakhla's rapid growth has been spurred by growing global demand for *O. vulgaris*. In addition to the industrial trawling going on offshore, a large fleet of thousands of artisanal fishermen set out each day from beaches around Dakhla in small wooden boats. They use pots and jigs to catch the cephalopod,[5] the same methods that have been used for catching octopuses for millennia and around the world. They go out alone, or with a small crew, and everyone works with their hands and their backs. Sometimes they are Sahrawi, born and raised in Dakhla, and sometimes they are men who have come south from other parts of Morocco to participate in this octopus rush, this boomtown bonanza. They make a frugal living at the bottom of the octopus's economic ladder, but it is more than they would make in their home towns. At the top of that economic ladder are factory ships with freezers on board under a variety of developed-world flags from Norway to Spain, which trawl the deeper waters off these coasts with nets dragged along the bottom, and sweep up octopus by the tonne to feed the global market.

For some years much of the world's supply of *O. vulgaris* came from the Atlantic, off the coasts of Spain and Portugal. This eastern Atlantic region, by itself, registered almost 100,000 tonnes during several years of production in the 1970s. Spain alone annually landed some 18,000 tonnes from 1967 to 1971, but in 1972 that number fell below 10,000 tonnes and has never recovered.[6] In 1983 a drastic drop – down to 48,000 tonnes – in the eastern

A Hawaiian octopus fishing lure, 1898.

Atlantic catch was reported.[7] Octopus catches continued to decline: by the year 2000, total global octopus production as reported to the FAO was under 35,000 tonnes.[8]

As octopus grew scarcer in the eastern Atlantic, industrial fishing vessels moved south to Morocco. Until 1987, according to a study published in *Fisheries Science*, the Moroccan octopus resource was underexploited, characterized by small catches and low prices. It then entered a 'maximum sustainable yield' stage in which the catch was moderate and the prices were not high, but were enough to mean octopus fishermen could realize a modest profit. From 1999 to 2001 the scale of the catch grew considerably, although prices remained about the same. From 2002 onwards the catch was small and prices were high.[9] The Moroccan government has had to impose increasingly severe restrictions on the octopus fishery.

Currently the Moroccan fishery is not enough to satisfy market demand, and the Mauritanian and Senegalese octopus fishing industries have grown rapidly over the past decade. Foreign factory trawlers pay Morocco, Mauritania or Senegal well for the right to fish off their shores, and stay at sea for six weeks at a time to capture hundreds of thousands of octopuses. When they finally fill their freezers, these ships bring their catch to large processing plants in the Canary Islands.

The drawback is that it appears to take relatively little time for these trawlers to negatively affect an octopus population. For example, the Mauritania catch dropped from 9,000 tonnes in 1993 to 4,500 tonnes in 2001. More recent studies conclude that octopus has hit an all-time low in the region, with 80 per cent less stocks than twenty years ago.[10] The stock continues to shrink, and is currently considered to be overfished by at least 33 per cent each year. By 2001 the Moroccan government was facing a drastic decline in its octopus fishery, and decided to impose two annual month-long closures on the octopus fishery during the two peak reproductive months, June and September.

Octopuses in Dakhla have not only played an economic role, but a political one. The octopus industry has been a vital part in a territorial war that the UN has categorized as one of the most intractable disputes in the world. The Western Sahara is the site of 40 years of struggle between Morocco and the Polisario Front, which is the party representing the region's indigenous population, the Sahrawi. These are a proud, independent desert people who rejected Spanish rule and the claims of sovereignty by Morocco to the north and Mauritania to the south in 1975. Polisario guerrilla attacks against both countries intensified in reaction to the Madrid Accord, a pact to end Spanish colonization there, and in 1978 Mauritania, mired in internal domestic strife, announced that it was withdrawing from the agreement. Morocco immediately claimed the abandoned territory as its own.

More than a dozen years of armed conflict with Polisario followed Mauritania's withdrawal, and an entire generation of

Togolese stamp celebrating Jules Verne's *Twenty Thousand Leagues under the Sea*.

Sahrawi was raised in exile, in refugee camps in the desert of western Algeria at Tinduf. A ceasefire was brokered in 1991 by the United Nations, and a referendum in the Western Sahara on the question of independence was scheduled, but more than twenty years later, after repeated postponements, it still had not been held. Meanwhile the Moroccan government 'encourages' people from poor areas of Morocco to settle in Dakhla and fish for octopus in anticipation of their votes in an eventual plebiscite.

Marches are held sporadically in Dakhla to protest Moroccan usurpation of the local octopus resource, and Moroccan response can be harsh. On 8 July 2008, for instance, Sahrawis demonstrated in Dakhla against the plundering of fish stocks in the territory by Morocco, and the presence of hundreds of unregistered octopus fishing boats manned by Moroccans, towards which the authorities turned a blind eye. Three weeks later thousands of Moroccans

Cephalopods are in steady demand in Barcelona's wholesale fish market.

were reported to have attacked Sahrawi fishermen with knives and axes in the fishing village of Itereft, an hour from Dakhla, injuring some 60 people. Observers speculated that the attack was meant to send a message throughout the region to Sahrawi octopus fishers, and to push them out of the Dakhla fishery.[11]

So goes life in Dakhla, where both Moroccan and Sahrawi fishermen try to eke out a living from putting in long, back-breaking hours in small boats. The Moroccans speak depreciatively of the Sahrawi as thieving and dishonest, and the natives say the same about the Moroccans, but when the wind is blowing hard off the desert, which is almost all the time, it is the real enemy. It kicks up high waves at sea that can overturn one of the brightly painted, wooden, 20-foot vessels in the blink of an eye. The ocean regularly swallows octopus fishermen, Moroccan and Sahrawi alike.

The Mexican octopus fishery, off the Yucatán coast, also loses men every year to its body of water – the Gulf of Mexico. Nevertheless the fishery has grown steadily over the past 50 years since an article in the *Bulletin of Marine Science* in 1966 described a new species of octopus, *Octopus maya*, captured in the Bay of Campeche off Mexico's Yucatán peninsula.[12] While it superficially resembled *O. vulgaris*, two things immediately differentiated it: a pair of double-ringed ocelli, and eggs that were substantially larger and less numerous than those of the common octopus. Its double-ringed ocelli gained it the nickname of '*pulpo de cuatro ojos*' ('four eyed octopus').

In 1993 the Mexican government imposed a restricted season for the octopus in order to assure that the population was undisturbed during its breeding season. It is still in effect, and the fishery operates from approximately 1 August to 15 December. Over the course of the 2011 season, in the states of Yucatán and Campeche, some 11.8 million kg (26 million lb) of octopus was

Easter Island rock carving of an octopus, 10th–12th century.

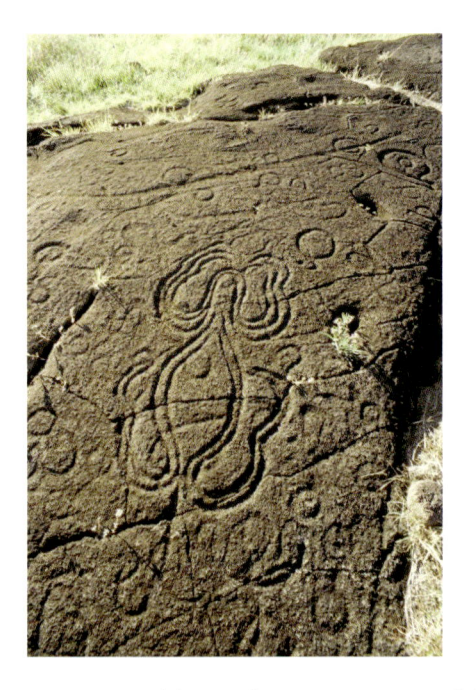

landed. Sixty per cent of that catch went to Europe, and the rest to Asia.[13]

In the Yucatán octopus fishermen work with *jimbas* (pronounced heem-ba), a curious tool for catching octopus said to have been invented by fishermen in nearby Campeche. A *jimba* is a thick, 7.5-m-long (24-foot) bamboo pole. Each *jimba* has four lines with weights on them, two at the front and two behind. At the end of each line a blue crab is tied. The *jimbas* extend beyond the boat, and the lines are lowered into the water, to the bottom. A *jimba* is not easy to use, and only long years of practice teach a fisherman the right technique. When a tug on one of the lines indicates that an octopus has enfolded a crab, the fisherman has to judge the right moment to pull up the line without dislodging the octopus. It has to be when the crab is firmly in the octopus's grasp, but before it has eaten too much. This method of fishing has various advantages: one is that it does not harm the octopus, meaning that undersize specimens can be tossed back to grow larger. Another advantage is that since a female stops eating when she is depositing eggs, there is little chance of catching a gravid female.

For many octopus fishermen in the small villages along the Yucatán coast, the six-month fishing season represents the high point of their annual interaction with a market economy. A season in which *O. maya* is scarce, or when a red tide – an explosion in population of algae – prevents the cephalopod's capture, means a hard year for many families. While people along this coast are

Cooking *Octopus maya* in the Yucatán town of Sisal.

adept at surviving in the environment around them, simple survival is not enough for anyone who aspires to more than a day-to-day existence for themselves and/or their children. Most people in these places grow up hoping to acquire a little piece of land with a rudimentary cement-block house on it, maybe a boat if they're lucky. They also have the knowledge of how to fish, hunt and prepare what's caught and killed, and how to extract sustenance from the place where they live, a body of knowledge that has accumulated over generations. That know-how will get a person from day to day, year after year, but does not go far when it comes to meeting unexpected expenses. A good octopus season can mean a big improvement over this meagre standard of living. More than 15,000 jobs along this coast are directly related to octopus, and in 2006 the annual value of the fishery was $36 million.[14]

The port of Progreso has fifteen octopus processing plants, which work around the clock during the fishing season. In 2011 the allowable total catch was set at almost 13,000 tonnes (11.8 million kg, or 26 million lb). It was a good season, with prices reaching record highs due to a poor season for *O. vulgaris* off the North African coast. The daily newspaper in Progreso reported that local businesses were seeing a notable upturn in consumer spending, particularly on big-ticket items like televisions, sound systems and washing machines.[15]

The Mediterranean is, of course, another source of product for the global octopus market. Over the centuries, people in all the countries with a Mediterranean coastline have fished for octopus and incorporated it into their diets. The ancient Greeks believed that coastal dwellers could occasionally even fish for them on dry land. Aristotle wrote that the octopus was the only marine creature to regularly leave the water, and for those lucky enough to live close to shore and who come on an octopus clinging to a

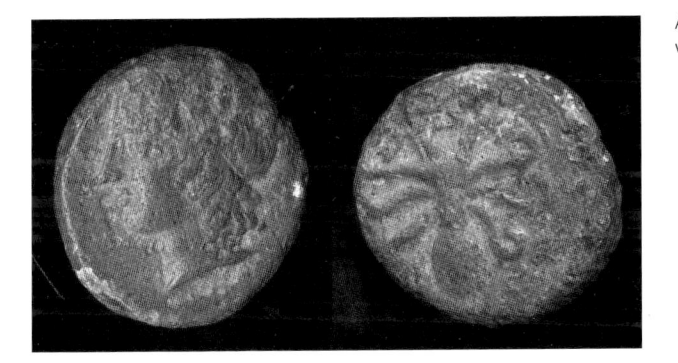

Ancient Greek coin with an octopus.

rock, he counselled that they save the trouble of trying to wrestle it free:

> The octopus, in fact, clings so tightly to the rocks that it cannot be pulled off, but remains attached even when the knife is employed to sever it; and yet, if you apply fleabane to the creature, it drops off at the very smell of it.[16]

The octopus coming ashore to steal food is a recurrent theme in the Mediterranean, and Pliny wrote in 77 CE of a giant octopus that came ashore to steal salted fish belonging to villagers. Oppian of Corycus reported around 170 CE that it was common for farmers in coastal areas to see octopuses in their olive trees at night. He wrote of the passion that octopuses feel for the grey-green foliage of the olive trees, and how wherever a particularly fine specimen grows close to the shore, an octopus will come out of the sea at night to embrace it, first entwining the trunk in its arms, then pulling itself up among the tree's branches. He went on to explain how fishermen took advantage of the octopus's passion for the olive tree:

Fishing boat with drying octopus, Greece.

As the twining ivy tendril clings about the tall fir-trees and, reaching forth from the root, climbs upwards and overruns the branches everywhere: so does the Poulpe [octopus] joyfully embrace the sleek branches of the olive and seems to kiss them. But when he has relieved his desire, he crawls back again to the bosom of the sea, having satisfied his love and longing for the olive. The snare of this same love is his undoing, as fishermen know. For they bind together well the branches of the olive and put in the midst thereof the lead, and tow them from the boat. The Poulpe, when he remarks it, is not unheeding but rushes to embrace his branchy comrades. And not even when he is being hauled to capture does he relax the bonds of desire, till he is within the boat, nor even while he perishes does he hate the olive.[17]

Whether or not fishermen in Oppian's day actually caught octopus by trailing a cluster of olive branches through the water, all the countries with a Mediterranean coastline seem to have always had artisanal octopus fisheries, and they persist to this day. Many of the methods of fishing used thousands of years ago are the same ones used today. With my own eyes I have watched as fishermen pulled up pots off the coast of Catalonia in which octopuses had made their homes, and which they were so loath to leave that they allowed themselves to be brought on deck and captured,[18] a process not so different from attracting them to branches and pulling them up. I have also seen men haul fyke nets with octopuses in them out of the waters around the Greek island of Ios; and jig them up while bent over the side of a rowing boat off the coast of a Balearic island using a homemade glass-bottomed box to spot octopuses on the sea floor, then putting the multi-hooked jig to them. Octopuses caught in pots, trapped or jigged still account for about half of the annual catch in the Mediterranean, while the rest is taken by bottom trawling.[19] The Mediterranean octopus fishery captured 15 tonnes each year between the mid-1980s and 2005.[20]

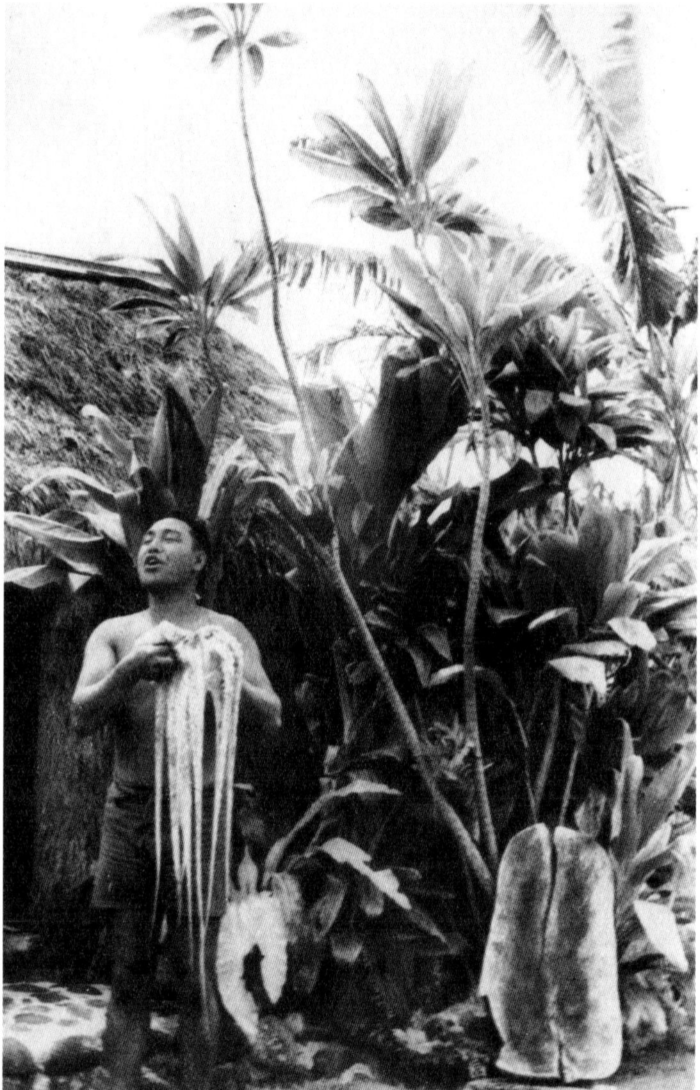

These octopuses are fresh out of the Mediterranean.

While numerous fisheries contribute to the global octopus commerce, one market, in particular, drives it: the Japanese market. Japan is the principal buyer of captured octopus in the world, importing an estimated 100,000 tonnes per year.[21] And, while Japanese people eat a lot of octopus, much of what gets bought is not for national consumption but is processed for sushi and shipped to Japanese restaurants in the U.S. and around the globe. All of the octopus sushi in the U.S., for instance, is sent from Japan, although it is by no means all caught there. It comes to Japan from other countries first – from Mauritania, Morocco,

Hawaiian man with octopus.

95

Netsuke of a fly on an octopus arm, 19th century.

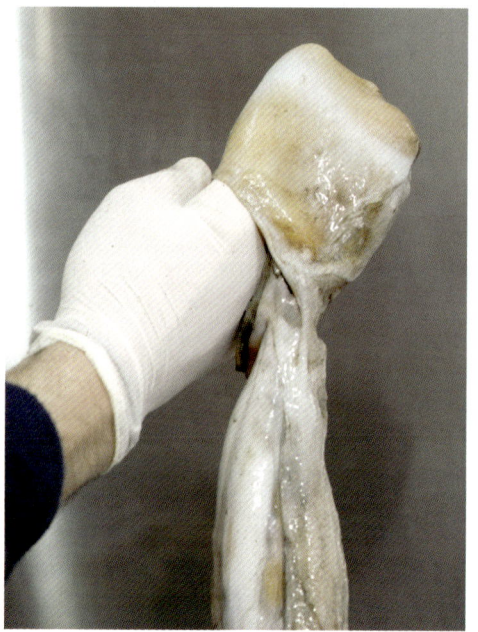

Anyone want to buy an octopus?

Spain, Vietnam or China – and is then sent on to the u.s. by Japanese exporters with plants in places like Kobe, its price rising with each stop along the route.

The best-tasting octopuses are those that come from Japanese waters, say aficionados, and many of these are reserved for domestic consumption, but not nearly enough of them are caught each year to satisfy local demand. The principal local octopus is the same species as that of the Atlantic and the Mediterranean, *O. vulgaris*, and the Japanese catch it primarily in the 450-km-long (280-mile) Seto Inland Sea. However the relatively small numbers of octopus taken annually out of the Seto Inland Sea are generally sold fresh to high-end restaurants or at local markets. What is caught there generally stays in Japan to be eaten by a lucky few who are able to pay for the pleasure. Even at top dollar, local octopuses are so scarce that fishing for

Prepared octopus on display in Japan.

初霜 起客

暖山の櫻とさらよ
ちかくりき
汐干の竜乃花貝

久堅屋

細ごさき
磯の汐干の
おとし
いかゆ
さらほ
蛸の
煮もお
さ

them is uncertain, and the number of people who do so at an artisanal level shrinks each year, mostly consisting of small fisheries that use strings of pots like those used in the Mediterranean; the fishermen are usually the descendants of fishing families who themselves are now growing elderly and whose numbers are winnowed by death each year. Few of their children choose to follow in their footsteps.

With both global demand and prices rising, it is not surprising that researchers and investors have been attracted to the idea of farming octopus. The problem with farming *O. vulgaris* is the 45–60 days that it spends as a planktonic paralarva, drifting in the water column. Scientists are still unsure about what it eats during this period, although the fact that it continues growing makes it clear that it is taking in some kind of nutrition. It has proven extremely tricky to keep the paralarvae alive until they enter the benthic stage and settle to the bottom. Substantial expenditures of both time and money to try and farm octopus have been made by Japan, Australia, Spain and Mexico.

With their tremendous commercial appetite for octopus, it is not surprising that the Japanese have tried to cultivate it. However, octopus farms have only been successful in rearing previously captured juveniles, which have already entered the benthic phase, to market size. Japanese hopes were raised in 1962 when researchers at the Hyogo Prefectural Fisheries Experimental Station took newly hatched larvae and raised them to the benthic stage for the first time, although they were only able to do so with a small fraction of any group of larvae, most of which died.[22] The mortality rate and the expense involved in raising those relatively few paralarvae to market size made the project financially unsustainable. Over the years no one has been able to overcome these problems, and in 2012 commercially feasible octopus aquaculture was still in the future.

Fishing for octopus, Japanese print, 1830.

Octopus for sale in a market in Korea.

Efforts to cultivate octopus are ongoing in Japan, but they are surrounded by secrecy and a dearth of published results. The company that manages to farm octopus stands to make a lot of yen. It is rumoured among octopus researchers in Spain and Mexico that Japanese researchers working for private firms may have successfully cultivated *O. vulgaris* and are now marketing it without noting that it is farm-raised, but so far nothing has been published on this development, and no one in the West is able to say for sure.

The Spanish, on the other hand, have been much more forthcoming about their efforts, and their failures, to farm *O. vulgaris*. Most of this research was concentrated in the Atlantic port city of Vigo in western Spain. From there, beginning in 2003, a series of optimistic reports were issued on the progress being made towards cultivating octopus (or *pulpo* in Spanish). But this early optimism proved to be premature. While octopuses were successfully raised in cages, the success was limited by the difficulty of growing paralarvae to a size where they could be put in cages, and by 2007 hopes for octopus farming had dimmed.[23]

Mexico is the only place to have had any real, demonstrable success at farming octopus, and that is primarily because the species being grown is *O. maya* and not *O. vulgaris*. It turns out that the most important difference between *maya* and *vulgaris* is neither egg size nor the rings around the creature's eyes, but rather the fact that *maya* does not pass through a planktonic, paralarval stage. Instead it hatches out as a tiny octopus that goes straight to the sea bottom and begins foraging for its food, as it will do for the rest of its life. A joint venture between a professor from the National Autonomous University of Mexico (UNAM) at a marine

A Catalan octopus fisherman boats another one.

research station in the small, coastal Yucatán fishing village of Sisal, and a cooperative of Mayan women, reached a point after five years' hard work when they were able to produce octopuses of marketable size from eggs.[24]

I was fortunate to share the moment. As we watched a couple of dozen octopuses being netted from their tanks in March 2010, the professor who had led the Octopus Program in Sisal, Carlos Rosas, was convinced the project was finally about to take off. A 50-year-old marine biologist, Rosas was excited, almost euphoric. 'This is the first time we've had a harvest with a systematic production', he told me.

> Before this it has been sporadic. If we can produce these, we can produce tens of thousands. I'm very moved, and very proud of the people who work here. Sometimes a researcher like myself can dream of things outside of reality, but here the people do not have that luxury. We've shown today that our project can work in the real world.[25]

The plan for the Octopus Program called for land adjoining UNAM's to be purchased by the Mayan women's cooperative with grants and business development loans, and turned into an octopus farm. It was to have 30 outdoor tanks for reproduction and fattening and indoor facilities for incubation and pre-fattening, along with a processing plant and a small restaurant. Patent revenues for the structural and infrastructural solutions devised in the process would be divided equally between the university and the cooperative.

Unfortunately the land where this complex was set to be built became the object of conflict between those who wanted to develop it for tourists and those who wanted to use it for growing octopuses. The project became embroiled in bureaucracy and bitterness between neighbours, and in August 2010 the building housing 13,000 octopuses, which were in the process of growing large enough to be transferred to the outside tanks, was burned to the ground.[26] The octopuses were killed and the installation destroyed. The fire was widely believed to have been set by someone who did not want to see the octopus farm prosper.

Slowly but surely, the cooperative's members are rebuilding, determined to carry on with their aquaculture. Is there a market for farm-raised *O. maya*? It will be a while before that question is answered, as the project had to start again from scratch in 2011, but they hope to have octopus ready for the market before the end of 2013.

Most octopus eaters say there is little or no difference between the taste or texture of *O. maya* and *O. vulgaris*, but many in the global market – from Manhattan to Tokyo – hold out for the common octopus, if only because that's what they're used to, according to Vincent Cutrone, owner of the Octopus Garden, a wholesaler of octopus to some of New York's finest restaurants. He is a short, trim, energetic man whose workday begins at 5 a.m. in Brooklyn, preparing the day's octopuses for shipment and loading them on delivery trucks. That night, they will grace the plates of people dining in some of New York's most exclusive restaurants. Cutrone told me he has yet to buy *O. maya*, because his customers want *O. vulgaris*.

> I've tried it, and I'm not sure there's any difference in taste. Maybe *vulgaris* is a little firmer. I don't know, but my customers are very specific: they want *Octopus vulgaris*, and the customer is always right.[27]

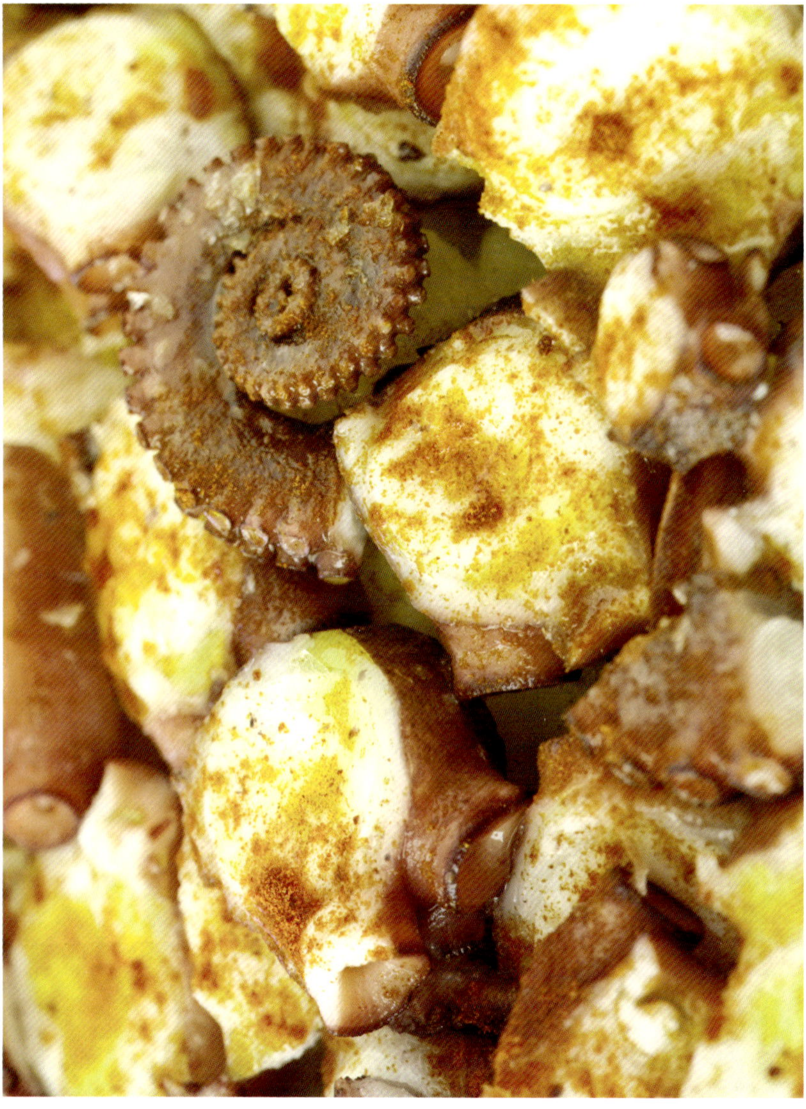

5 Octopus Cuisine

There is very good octopus on the coast of Campeche.
Diego de Landa, *An Account of the Things of Yucatán* (1572)

One place where there's no problem convincing someone to eat *Octopus maya* is in the Yucatán, where they catch them. The principal dishes in which octopuses are served are *pulpo en su tinta*, octopus in its own ink; in *escabeche*, which is a vinegary preparation; in *mojo de ajo*, which is prepared with oil and garlic; and served raw as *ceviche*. Take your pick; they are all delicious, surprisingly tender and tasty. Perhaps the best I ever ate was the freshly caught octopus that a friend in Sisal cooked in its own juices over a charcoal fire outdoors in a blackened pan before cutting it into thin slices and serving with rice, beans and a homemade habanero chilli sauce. I have had the good fortune to eat a lot of *O. maya*, and for my money, regardless of what New York chefs may say, it is tastier than its Mediterranean cousin.

Don't waste your breath trying to tell that to the octopus buyer for Barcelona's Pulpería Bar Celta, however. This hole-in-the-wall tapas bar on a narrow medieval street in Barcelona serves up to 6,800 kg (15,000 lb) of octopus a year. Octopus is the star of the Pulpería's menu, as its name implies, but there's only one way it is served, and that's as *pulpo a la gallega*, Galician style. Not only is *Octopus vulgaris* the only species used, but it must have been caught in the eastern Atlantic Ocean. Anything else is below the bar's standards. 'We won't even buy octopus caught in

Octopus, Galician style.

the Mediterranean', says Luis, who has run the Pulpería's kitchen for seventeen years. 'The important thing is not whether it comes from the Atlantic waters off Galicia or Portugal or Morocco or Mauritania, what matters is that it's from the Atlantic and not the Mediterranean. It tastes better.'[1]

The bar is close to the port, and offers an array of tapas, but the signature dish is *pulpo a la gallega*. It is remarkably simple to prepare, but delicious served with some fresh, crusty, local bread. 'Once we defrost the octopus and make sure it's clean, we put it in boiling water, and once the water is boiling again leave it in there for thirty minutes', says Luís. 'Then, cut it and serve it on a wooden plate, topped with paprika, high-quality olive oil, and a good table salt, and that's it. It doesn't get any better.'

People have expressed similar feelings about eating octopus for millennia. In ancient Greek and Roman banquets cephalopods – squid, cuttlefish and octopus – were common, according to Frank Lane, who wrote that octopus and squid were often sent as a gift on the fifth day after the birth of a child. The food historian Andrew Dalby confirms this, noting that the menu for a typical *Amphidromia* (a baby's naming day, held five or ten days after birth) was recorded by Ephippus around 370 BCE:

> The custom is to bake slices of Chersonese cheese, to fry cabbage gleaming with oil, to stew some fat mutton chops, to pluck wood-pigeons and thrushes along with chaffinches, to nibble little cuttlefish along with squids, to swing and beat many [an octopus] tentacle, and to drink many a warming cup.[2]

Octopus, according to Dalby, was also considered by the Greeks to be an aphrodisiac. He records that Athenaeus cited the comic playwright Alexis on the matter: 'Octopus increases sexual vigour,

An elegant octopus in a mosaic at the ancient Roman town Herculaneum.

but it is tough and indigestible. The larger species provide better nourishment. When boiled slowly, it settles the stomach and moistens the bowel.'[3]

Pliny the Elder tells us that the Romans delighted in eating octopus and, according to an article by Paul Bartsch in the annual *Report of the Smithsonian Institute* for 1916, they used bamboo knives rather than metal ones to slice them, because they felt the metal added an unpleasant flavour to the delicacy. The same article recounts the story of the Greek Philoxenu of Leucas, who lived around 400 BCE. One night he had a huge octopus for dinner, finishing the entire thing except for the head, and then fell ill. When he was told by his physician that his gluttony would probably result in his death within a few hours, he called for the

Octopus drying on a clothesline in Greece.

head, and when he had eaten it he lay down to die, saying that now he had nothing left in this world to regret.[4]

Another famous Greek who may have met his end over an octopus is Diogenes, the wonderful Cynic philosopher who was born around 410 BCE in modern-day Sinop in Turkey, an Ionian colony on the Black Sea. He lived to be almost 90 before dying at Corinth in 323 BCE. Various accounts of how he died exist, but the two most often cited are that he ate a raw octopus and died of colic,[5] or that he was dividing an octopus for his dogs to eat and one of them bit him on the foot; the wound became infected and killed him.

Marcus Gavius Apicius was another of history's famous gourmands, or gluttons. He was a Roman who lived in the first century CE, during the reign of Tiberius. Pliny the Elder wrote of his epicurean tastes: 'Apicius, the most gluttonous gorger of all spendthrifts, established the view that the flamingo's tongue has an especially fine flavour.'[6] A collection of recipes gathered some 400 years after his death, but not in fact written by him, was titled *Apicius*, or *De re coquinaria* (*On the Subject of Cooking*). After being passed down through the centuries, it was printed for the first time in 1506. It provides a window into what people were eating in a declining Roman Empire. *De re coquinaria* recommends cooking octopus with pepper, lovage, sauce and ginger. The sauce was likely to have contained numerous ingredients, including the most popular of Rome's condiments, *garum*, a fermented fish sauce.[7]

What people ate during the Dark Ages was not gathered up and recorded in recipe books. Once the Dark Ages faded into the Renaissance, however, recipes quickly became a popular subject for printing. One of the earliest available in manuscript form in the mid-fourteenth century – was the collection *Llibre de Sent Soví*, written in Catalan by an anonymous cook thought to have been a priest or a nobleman – someone in the kingdom of Aragon with time and resources enough to create a book of recipes dedicated to St Salvio.[8] Among its 72 recipes is one for octopus, which calls for making a stuffing for an octopus out of its own arms cut

Minoan frieze of an octopus at Knossos.

up with parsley, mint, 'and other good herbs', along with garlic, onion and raisins, and cooking it over hot coals, or in an oven.[9] The first printed recipe book in Catalan, the *Llibre del coch*, was compiled by Robert de Nola in the early sixteenth century. It had only one recipe for a dish prepared in an oven, and that was for baked octopus.

Bartolomeo Scappi was another famous medieval chef and cookbook author. Born in Lombardy, Italy, around 1500, he served as a chef at the Vatican for popes Pius IV and Pius V. Before that he was in the service of one Cardinal Lorenzo Campeggio. He first made his name then by organizing a banquet the Cardinal hosted for Charles v at which some 800 dishes were served. In 1570, two years before his death, he published in Venice his *Work on the Art of Cooking* (*Opera dell'arte del cucinare*), which contained around 1,000 recipes. By 1612 it had been translated into Spanish and Dutch. He recommends boiling an octopus in water and salt, then cutting it into small pieces to fry in oil. When done, serve it with a sauce, or with pimento, salt and the juice of sour oranges.

On the other side of Spain from its Mediterranean coast, in Galicia on the Atlantic Ocean, octopus is believed to have been eaten since prehistoric times, according to anthropologist José Antonio Fidalgo Santamariña. Exactly how long people in this region have been eating octopus is hard to measure precisely, since the octopus has no bones and leaves very little in the way of archaeological remains. While octopus certainly was initially the food of coastal dwellers, it was brought inland early on the backs of mules by traders. Muleteers would carry products from inland Galicia,

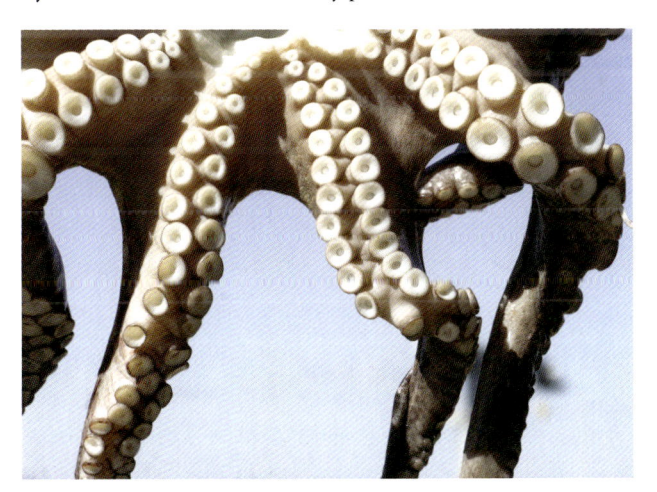

Arms, not tentacles.

Catania fish market, Sicily, December 2012.

such as cheese and potatoes, to the coast, where they would sell them, and return with dried octopus and fish to sell inland.

In medieval Galicia, when the Church was the region's largest landholder, peasants worked the land and paid annual tributes to the monasteries and convents to which it belonged. This was frequently paid, at least partly, in the currency of dried octopus, as records show from as early as the mid-fifteenth century. Racks on which to dry octopus can still be spotted outside farmhouses along the Galician coast.

By the eighteenth century many marketplaces in Galicia included among their butchers, fishmongers and vegetable vendors someone who prepared and sold octopus, a *pulpeiro* if a man, or *pulpeira* if a woman. In 1752 in the town of San Xoán de Arcos, out of 102 heads of family, 48 were labourers, 39 were tanners, nineteen were cobblers and nine were vendors of octopus who travelled from market to market.

Since then the octopus has never fallen out of favour in Galicia, although it is no longer prepared from dried. These days, if not eaten fresh, it is frozen and eaten later. To appreciate the Galician appetite for octopus, the best time to visit is during the octopus festival in the town of O Carballiño. A dozen neighbours got together in 1964 for the first of the fiestas honouring the octopus, and in 50 years it has grown to be one of Galicia's largest and most important festivals. By 2010 the festival had gained an international reputation, and nearly 45,000 kg (100,000 lb) of octopus was consumed each year by some 70,000 visitors on the second Sunday of every August. Each year tens of thousands of people fill a park in the centre of town to enjoy *pulpo a la gallega*. The other components of the day's octopus-centred meal include the Galician country bread called *pan de Cea* and a regional Ribeiro wine.[10]

On the southern side of the Mediterranean, the octopus has also been avidly consumed, presumably since time immemorial, although the written record is scant. Henry Lee records that in nineteenth-century Tunis, according to a report from W. Kirby

Pen-and-ink drawing by Albert Flamen, mid-17th century.

Green, who was British consul there in 1872, the residents of the island of Kerkennah would build long weir-like structures out of palm branches in which they would capture tons of octopus. These were cleaned, boiled and shipped in oil or brine via Malta to Greece, where they had long held a special place for members of the Greek Orthodox Church who made octopus a basis of their Lenten diet.[11]

My own preferred way to cook octopus was passed along to me by a Catalan octopus fisherman, Pere Pau Gras, whose home port is the coastal town of Sant Carles de la Ràpita. His recipe for octopus stew didn't sound appetizing when he gave it to me, but served with fresh bread it's hard to beat. First take an octopus that's been frozen for at least a week and defrost it. Cut the arms into inch-long pieces. Then sauté some onions, garlic and grated tomato in a good olive oil. Add most of a can of beer and let the mixture boil. Put the pieces of arms in and bring it back to a boil, then let it simmer for fifteen minutes. Toss in three or four potatoes, cut in quarters, and let it simmer for another fifteen minutes.

For all its remarkable traits – intelligence, camouflage and so on – what most people, most of the time, in most places, think of when they think of an octopus is a meal, and nowhere in the world is octopus consumed with greater relish than in Japan. Octopus consumption per capita there is far and away the highest in the world, and in no part of Japan is it higher than among people who live close by the Seto Inland Sea. On the island of Awaji, for instance, close to the cities of Kobe and Osaka, the octopus is omnipresent. It is immediately and frequently evident in everything from the economy, to household decorations, to the name of the ferry boat linking the island to the mainland, to an amazing number of ways to prepare all sizes of octopus for the table. It is sold from pushcarts on the street simmered in soy sauce and sugar, dried and seasoned in strips, as octopus balls or as deep-fried octopus kebabs. The island is not remote – it is connected to Kobe on one end by the longest suspension bridge in the world, over the Akashi Straits, and on the other end towards Osaka – but it does have its own history and culture, and particularly its own relationship to *tako*, the octopus. What's more, Japanese gourmets unanimously agree that the octopus caught off the shores of Awaji are the tastiest in Japan.

The region is famous for a number of octopus dishes, including sashimi, tempura, *takowasa* (raw octopus marinated in wasabi), and *tako no nitsuke*, which is a bit of octopus poached in a salty-sweet mixture of sugar, soy sauce and ginger. Another traditional speciality is *takoyaki*, a kind of octopus dumpling made from a tiny piece of boiled octopus arm tucked inside a light ball of dough with a little pickled ginger and spring onion. It is prepared in a special grill, and is a popular street food throughout the area. A *takoyaki* grill is as common in an Osaka home's kitchen as a waffle iron in Kansas. The golf-ball-sized pastries are served with a variety of dipping sauces. A street vendor named Endo Tomekichi, from Osaka, is said to have created *takoyaki* in 1935, and the snack he invented became emblematic of Osaka and can now be found across Japan. While it was long seen in Tokyo as a kid's snack, by 2002 the city was full of *takoyaki* shops. A survey made in 2001 by the *Japan Times*, for instance, found six shops within a 200-yard radius of the train station in the Shimokitazawa neighbourhood.[12]

Hamako nabe is a dish of octopus, oysters and other fresh seafood and vegetables boiled in a miso-based soup. It is named after '*hamako*' (people who worked at salt farms) and is a speciality of the town of Setoda-cho on Ikuchi island in the Seto Inland Sea, in the Onomichi area of Hiroshima. Octopus salad, *tako su*, is common, as are octopus sashimi and octopus sushi, although unlike much sashimi and sushi using other species, the octopus is not served raw, but has been softened by boiling.

Reporting from Akashi – a port on the sheltered sea between the main islands of Honshu and Shikoku – Yasushi Wada wrote in the *Yomiuri Shimbun*,

> To overcome the summer's enervating heat, Kansai folk have a recipe – serve up octopus. So popular is the belief in the Kansai region that consuming octopus is effective in relieving fatigue that July 2 unofficially has been named Day of the Octopus . . .
>
> 'Octopus can be caught throughout most of the year off Akashi, but it tastes best from July to the Bon season in August', said Yosuke Maeda, an employee of the Akashiura fisheries cooperatives. 'In summer, shrimps and crabs, the favourite foods of octopuses, are abundant. So octopuses caught around this time are most delicious.' The current is strong in this area, which makes octopuses chewy and tastier . . .
>
> The city's specialty is egg dumplings, better known as Akashiyaki outside the city. Whereas the better-known takoyaki dumplings are typically filled with octopus, vegetables and tempura scraps, Akashiyaki dumplings contain only octopus. Another difference is that takoyaki are consumed with a savoury sweet sauce, while Akashiyaki dumplings are dipped in a dashi broth made from kombu [dried kelp] and katsuobushi [dried bonito flakes] . . . Unlike takoyaki with its heavily seasoned flavour, Akashiyaki dumplings have a simple taste, making the flavour of the octopus stand out.[13]

Takoyaki stand in Osaka, Japan.

コナモンミュージアム
Dotonbori Konamon-Museum
入口
O-NIKO
たこ焼
実演中
500円
くくる
明石焼
専門店
B1F

Akashi is famous all over Japan for its octopuses. In a *Huffington Post* piece the late food writer Alan Davidson related a local legend that once upon a time a monster octopus living off the coast of Akashi stretched its arms on to the land and harassed a princess resting in a palace nearby. This prompted the people to devise the *tako-tsubo* (octopus-pot) method for catching octopuses. Long, narrow earthenware pots tied with ropes are lowered to the seabed and later, when octopuses are comfortably settled in them, lifted out of the water. The seabed along the coast of Hyōgo Prefecture is divided neatly into plots, and each octopus-fisher of the area is allowed to sink his octopus-pots only into his plot – an ancient right that is jealously guarded.[14]

In Japan two common ways of cooking octopus are boiling and *nimono*. For the former technique, a live octopus is chosen, cleaned, boiled just lightly in order to prevent it from getting tough, and then sliced thin and eaten with a dipping sauce made variously with soy sauce, citrus juice or wasabi. For *nimono*, it is

Japanese netsuke of an octopus, early 19th century, lacquered wood.

simmered for hours, often with vegetables. However the Japanese eat octopus prepared in numerous ways apart from these, including octopus ice cream, fried octopus crackers and octopus flavoured crisps.

Octopus has been prepared for the table in many different ways across the centuries, and around the world, but one basic culinary rule has always applied everywhere: they are not suitable for human consumption until they are tenderized. 'The octopus must be beaten with twice seven blows' is an ancient Greek proverb, according to Dalby.[15] I saw my first octopus in 1968, and, indeed, it was being beaten against a bit of rocky shore on the Greek island of Ios by a stocky woman in a black dress with her sleeves rolled up. She had hold of one of its arms and was swinging it through the air and down on the rocks at the edge of the Aegean Sea, again and again, just as women had done before her for millennia.

The Japanese beat an octopus with a mallet before cooking it; Spaniards traditionally recommend dipping it in boiling water three times, then cooking it in a copper pot; and Italians are said to boil it with a cork in the belief that enzymes in the cork tenderize it. What Vincent Cutrone does is put his octopuses into a machine at the back of his Brooklyn seafood market, the Octopus Garden. It is essentially a stainless steel tub with two paddles mounted inside, driven by a motor. Salt and water are added, sloshing back and forth, as the paddles thump the octopus. The first of these mechanical tenderizing devices were converted washing machines (top-loaded octopuses!), but the salt water corroded their parts, and thus the use of stainless steel. 'What I do in this tub is the equivalent of beating an octopus on the rocks', he told me, when he showed me his octopus tenderizing machine.

We defrost the octopuses, clean them, and put them in the machine. We cover them with water, and add salt and ice. You can regulate the wave size of the water in there. Roughly a half hour later we'll change the water, and we'll do that until the new water stays clear and the octopus curls up beautifully.[16]

Fortunately for the home cook, particularly those who live in apartments with no convenient place to beat an octopus, freezing has no effect on its flavour, and is a perfectly good means of tenderizing it. In fact, simply freezing for a week or more, defrosting and cooking for the proper length of time, will produce an octopus that is eminently edible; less tough, say, than a good steak. However, Cutrone is convinced that the extra tenderizing his machine does is one of the main reasons he has become New York City's most highly regarded octopus wholesaler at a time when the city's top chefs are clamouring for octopus.

It is a good time to be selling octopus wholesale, because the cephalopod's popularity among foodies has risen rapidly. *Food Republic*, a website established in 2010, provides a good example. The site describes itself as 'founded on the idea that guys everywhere are putting food at the centre of their lives like never before. This is the site for men who want to eat and drink well, and to live smart.' A recent piece on the site stated, 'We are in the Golden Age of Octopus. It's not clear exactly when it happened, but seemingly out of nowhere, octopus popped up on the menu of every chef-driven restaurant in America.'[17]

Cutrone agrees. 'Octopus sales have just exploded', he told me. 'I have customers as far away as the MGM Grand in Las Vegas, in Atlanta, in Florida, and Bermuda. All of this has happened by word of mouth. And, in New York, it's unbelievable how many restaurants want octopus now.' Wholesale is only part of his

Grilled octopus can be tender and tasty.

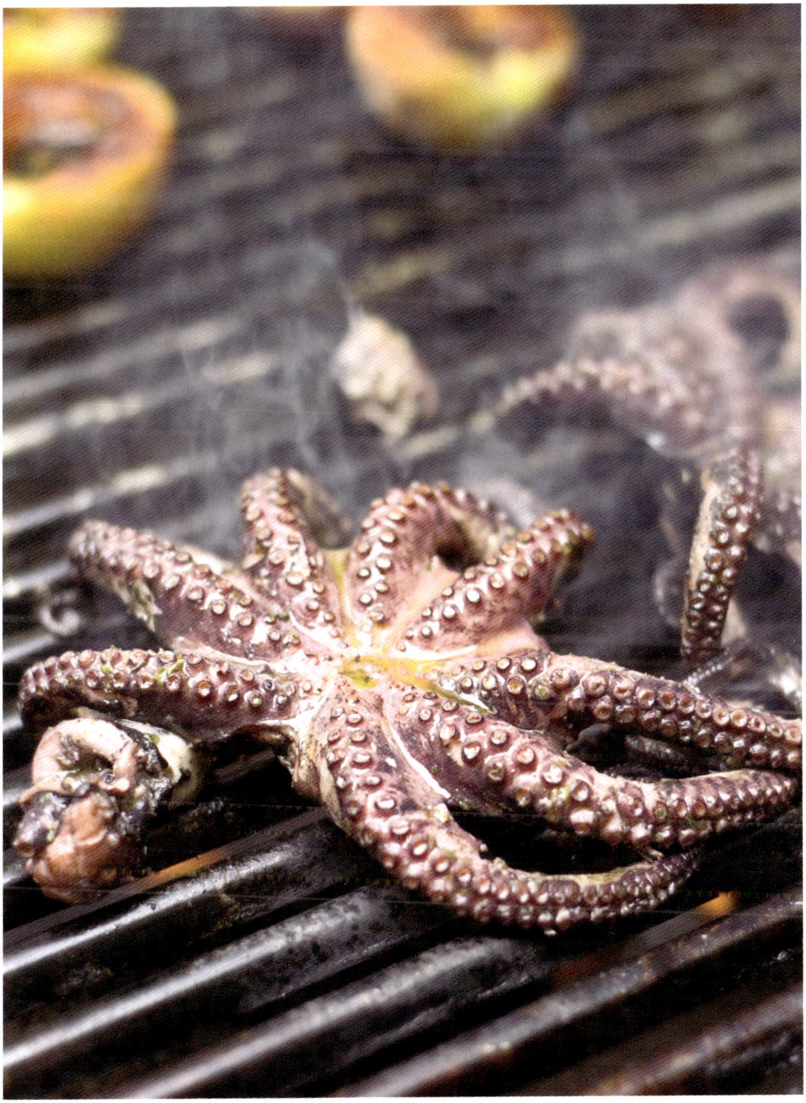

business. The front part of Octopus Garden is occupied by a butcher's white enamel display case, inside which, on a bed of ice, are three sizes of octopuses – babies of a couple of ounces, 7-ounce (200-g) youngsters, one of which fits nicely on a dinner plate, and big 4-pounders (1.8 kg). Cutrone displays them all on the ice with their arms 'curled up beautifully' under their bodies. A steady flow of customers comes through the door and most of the retail business is conducted in Italian. Cutrone arrived in the U.S. when he was fourteen, in 1974. He came from Bari on the Adriatic coast of Italy, and the way he ate octopus there is the same way his customers eat it here in Brooklyn's Bensonhurst neighbourhood.

Every 4 July he sets up in a nearby park and grills octopus for his neighbours to celebrate Independence Day.

> They line up for it. I make my grill very hot. The octopus has the guts and the beak taken out, and I open it up and put it down on the grill, pretty flat. When it changes colour, and I see it's done, I put it in a good olive oil and lemon juice, and it draws them up. It's delicious. You can even make sandwiches with it.[18]

Many of the Italian Americans living in Vincent Cutrone's neighbourhood view octopus as a comfort food and eat it regularly, but for most other North Americans it's as exotic and unthinkable a meal as scorpions or snakes. That anyone would pay good money to eat an octopus seems inexplicable to those who have never tasted one. Its appearance certainly does not say 'Eat me' to someone who has never had the pleasure, nor the opportunity. Often the reaction to considering an octopus as food has varied between polite disgust and outright revulsion. Such reactions are frequently reinforced when inept cooks, or those who simply have no experience with octopus, fail to tenderize them sufficiently before cooking.

Henry Lee recounted being served an octopus that had not first been beaten or tenderized in any manner:

> I shall never forget the utter loathing, ludicrously mingled with determination to conquer or conceal that feeling, which was depicted on the countenances of some of the guests at a memorable 'octopus-lunch' given by my friend Sir John Cordy Burrows at Brighton, in 1874.
>
> His cook had never before prepared an octopus, and was, probably, not well pleased to do so then. The nasty-looking object was placed on the table in all its undisguised ugliness. Its skin, which in the process of boiling had become lividly purple, and had not been removed, was in places offensively broken and abraded; and its arms, shrivelled and shrunk, sprawled helplessly on the dish, and,

Octopus swimming.

somehow, looked, as they proved to be, as tough and ropy as so many thongs of hunting-whips. Our genial host saw in an instant that it was a failure in cookery, but, as usual, he was equal to the occasion. With a twinkle of his eye he took a sly glance at me, and gravely handed a portion of the octopus to an honoured guest. 'Now, sir', said he, 'just taste that, and enjoy one of the luxuries of the ancient Greeks!'

. . . I helped him and myself to some of the most approved portions of the leathery creature. Manfully and perseveringly for some minutes I tried to masticate a mouthful of it, but it was useless; and feeling that if human teeth could make no more impression on it than on the sole of an old boot, the human stomach incurred risk of difficulties which all the well-known medical skill of our good host might be unable to cure, I declined to sacrifice myself to an idea, and, well, I did not swallow it.[19]

The fact that many people perceived the octopus as somewhat repulsive was one of the things that endeared it to Eric Ripert, the superstar chef at Manhattan's Le Bernardin who won the James Beard Foundation award for Outstanding Chef of the Year in 2003. When I spoke with him in 2007, his menu offered octopus as a prelude to the main dish. 'At Le Bernardin I always like to have a raw or marinated fish to begin with, and then something which is sometimes a little bit adventurous for the client, before they have something more substantial', he told me.

One of Cutrone's 6- to 8-ounce animals, beautifully curled up on a plate in all its octopus glory, worked just right in Ripert's 'adventurous' category, he said.

> I want to serve it as an octopus. To see the entire animal like that is slightly freaky, but at the same time it's a delight. If

you're eating octopus you have to be able to handle it, and if you're able to handle it, it looks beautiful on the plate like that . . . We're not going to slice it and hide its nature, we're saying, 'Look, it's right here.'[20]

The resulting dish was described on Le Bernardin's menu as 'braised baby octopus, black trumpet mushroom and truffle purée in a red wine and ink sauce infused with *herbes de Provence*'. Eric Ripert reckoned that he was serving fifteen to twenty a day. The dish was prepared by slowly braising the octopus in a broth of squid ink, red wine, chorizo sausage, Provençal herbs and lots of garlic for close to two hours. The result was served on the mushroom and truffle purée, and was remarkably tender and flavourful, with the chorizo providing a background to the octopus, everything combining in a rich, full meld of flavours and textures.

6 Octopus Iconography

Lying on her back, the woman leans back, supported at the waist and buttocks by the knees and thighs of her partner. The man lifts her waist to change the angle and the depth of penetration. The man can free one hand to caress his partner's breasts.
'The Octopus', from *Las Posturas del amor* ('The Positions of Love')

Eros and Thanatos, desire and death, are two of life's deepest mysteries. Over the past 200 years the octopus has served to symbolize both in the Western world, as it still does today. It was seen by the likes of Pablo Picasso as a sensuous creature, vital and pleasure-loving, while Victor Hugo drew an unforgettable portrait of the octopus as a ravening and implacable monster, bringer of death and destruction.

For Picasso and numerous other visual artists of his day, the artistic concept of the octopus was based on a coloured woodblock print made by the immensely talented Japanese artist Katsushika Hokusai in 1814, and widely circulated in Europe during the latter half of the nineteenth century. Known as *The Dream of the Fisherman's Wife*, it shows a Japanese woman, no longer young but still in the fullness of her body, lying with her legs spread open while an octopus performs cunnilingus between them, and a smaller octopus uses its arms to support her neck and caress her breasts. Her mouth is slightly open in pleasure, and she grips the arms of the larger octopus, pulling his mouth even further into her body. The octopus's huge, impassive eyes watch her face in its transport of pleasure. It is a deeply erotic scene, with a power that leaps off the page.

Hokusai's work is in the long tradition of *shunga*, the explicit Japanese woodblock prints that some call pornographic, and others see as erotic art. *Shunga* has its roots in the eleventh century, and was well developed by the time Europeans discovered it. Early French travellers to Japan, in particular, seem to have been enamoured of the *shunga* they saw, and began bringing prints back to Europe in the mid-1800s. One of the early owners of the Hokusai print was Edmond de Goncourt, a close friend of Victor Hugo, who began collecting *shunga* in 1863. By the 1880s he had amassed a sizeable collection. *Shunga* paid respect to this all-important part of life shared by humans everywhere in graphic, delightful detail, with a touch of humour and another of style, and it was a revelation to European artists and art lovers. Picasso and the artists around him in Barcelona, and later in Paris, were tremendously influenced by these works, and the most influential of these were Hokusai's.

Goncourt recorded in his journal a visit made by the sculptor Auguste Rodin to view his *shunga* collection:

> Rodin, who is full of faunishness, asks to see my Japanese erotics, and he is full of admiration before the women's drooping heads, the broken lines of their necks, the rigid extension of arms, the contractions of feet, all the voluptuous and frenetic reality of coitus, all the sculptured twining of bodies melted and interlocked in the spasm of pleasure.[1]

Other artists and writers who are known to have admired and possessed *shunga* were Aubrey Beardsley, Gustav Klimt, Émile Zola and Henri de Toulouse-Lautrec. As early as 1903, at the age of 21, Pablo Picasso executed a pencil and brown ink drawing he called *An Erotic Drawing: Woman and Octopus*, in which a mollusc – to tell the truth, it looks more like a cuttlefish than an octopus – pleasures a naked woman who is reclining and is willingly opening herself up to the animal's arms.

Katsushika Hokusai, *The Dream of the Fisherman's Wife*, 1814, coloured woodblock print.

In the octopus's transformation into symbol, some saw desire, others death. Not everyone was willing to concede that the woman in Hokusai's woodblock was *enjoying* the experience of oral sex with an octopus. More than one hidebound, guilt-ridden, male Western observer, unable to read the woodblock's sexually explicit Japanese text, did not see Hokusai's work for the erotic paean to the octopus that it was. Instead what they saw was a scene of rape and violation; rather than transports of ecstasy in the fisherman's wife's face, they saw horror, terror, a grimace of pain as the large octopus feasted on her genitalia, its huge eyes watching merciless, unmoved by her suffering.

That was the description of Hokusai's creation given by the art critic Joris-Karl Huysmans when he wrote about Japanese woodblocks:

The most beautiful print I know of in this genre is terrifying. A Japanese woman is mounted by an octopus; with its tentacles, the horrible beast sucks the tips of her breasts and burrows into her mouth, whilst with its head it feeds on her nether regions. The almost superhuman expression of anguish and pain which convulses the long Pierrot-like figure, with her aquiline nose, and the hysterical joy simultaneously conveyed by her forehead and her eyes closed as though in death, are admirable.[2]

Nothing promoted the image of wild, savage octopus as an implacable foe to humans as much as Victor Hugo's novel, *Les Travailleurs de la mer* (*The Toilers of the Sea*, 1866), which was translated into English that same year and was an international

Erotic *shunga* art with octopus.

bestseller. Its most riveting and dramatic scene features a tremendous battle between the hero, Gilliatt, and a ferocious octopus of terrifying dimensions which Hugo nicknames the 'devil-fish'. It is a merciless and bloodthirsty foe, wrote Hugo. The suckers are represented as being 'like so many lips trying to drink your blood . . . they bury themselves to the depth of an inch in the flesh of their prisoner . . . on contact with them your muscles swell, the fibbers are wrenched, and your blood gushes forth, and mixes horribly with the lymph of the mollusc'. He spends pages describing the imagined horrors of which the animal is capable, and concludes:

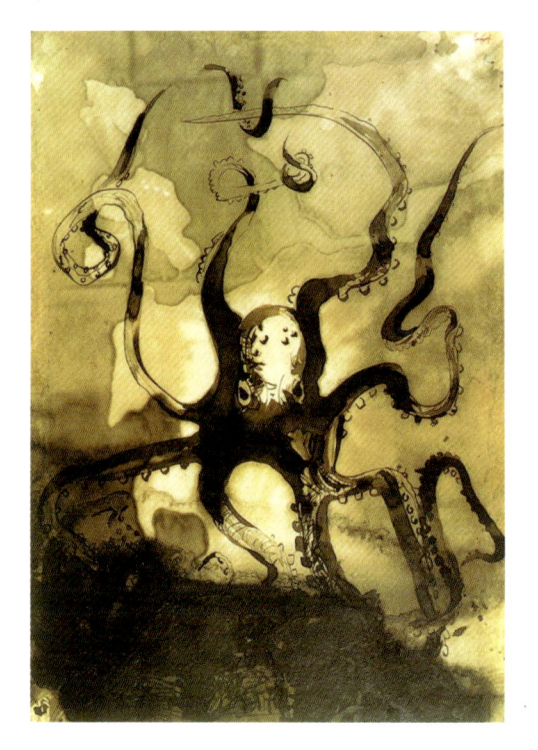

Victor Hugo, ink drawing of an octopus making his initials, c. 1866.

> They are the chosen forms of evil . . . They are as the darkness converted into beasts . . . These animals are phantoms as much as monsters. They are the amphibice of death, the visible extremities of black circles. They mark the transition of our reality to another.

The struggle between Gilliatt and the octopus is depicted in Hugo's most fulsome prose and the bestselling editions had a remarkable set of illustrations by Gustave Doré. For Hugo's readers across the Western world, the etching of Gilliatt's horrific eight-armed enemy, the 'devil-fish', latched on to a struggling, brave hero was what came to mind when they thought of an octopus.

The prose that accompanied the illustrations was no less horrifying:

> Orpheus, Homer and Hesiod imagined only the Chimera. God made the octopus. When He so wishes, God excels in the execrable. The wherefore of this perplexes the religious thinker. If terror were the object of its creation, the octopus is a masterwork. The whale has enormous bulk, the octopus is small. The hippopotamus has a hide, the octopus has no armour . . . The crocodile has its jaws full of teeth, the octopus has no teeth. The octopus has no muscular mass, no menacing cry, no armour, no horn, no dart, no claw, no tail with which to hold or bruise; no cutting fins or wings with nails, no spines, no sword, no electric discharge, no virus, no poison, no talons, no beak, no teeth. Yet he is of all creatures the most formidably armed. What then is the octopus? It is the sea vampire.[3]

Victor Hugo's conception of the octopus as evil incarnate, an implacable foe of human beings, resonated with many people.

Aboriginal bark drawing of octopus.

A part of us fears otherness, anything so different from us that we cannot know it or even imagine it. An octopus is such a vastly other creature that Hugo's portrayal of the animal as a monster was very powerful. In 1904, for instance, a writer and fellow of the Royal Geographic Society named Frank Thomas Bullen wrote:

> The sombre brown of its body, the pustular skin, the eyes in which a whole inferno of hatred of everything living seems to be concentrated, the palpitating orifice at the top of the head, opening now and then, sufficiently to show the parrot-like beak common to all the race, these are grisly features, but the eight arms, writhing, curling, clinging like a Medusa's hair, are features of the octopus which hold the imagination captive . . . as with the alligator, the mosquito, and the louse, since the Lord has seen fit to create him and place him in his present position, it does not become short-sighted man to question that Supreme Wisdom.[4]

The octopus is perceived negatively in this way because it is viewed by men as a symbol of a woman with a penis, according to Jacques Schnier, a psychoanalytic researcher who wrote an article in the mid-1950s about the symbolism of octopus through the ages, beginning with the common octopus motif found on Mycenaean pottery, produced between 1600 BCE and 1000 BCE. From our remove, thousands of years later, we cannot be sure what the octopus meant to the Mycenaeans, Schnier concedes, but we can see that over the centuries it became less realistic and figurative and much more abstract; more a symbol than a representation.

What we can examine is why modern Westerners have so often found the octopus a fearful creature, writes Schnier. He concludes that this negative perception of the octopus is because men view it, subconsciously, as a symbol of Greek mythology's Medusa, just as Bullen did in the extract above. Medusa's hair of writing snakes, symbolized by the octopus's eight arms, is actually a fantasy of a woman with a penis, according to Schnier, which in turn represents a fear of castration. Once we have understood this, he concludes, it is possible to conjecture that it meant

Political cartoon of 1914 showing President Woodrow Wilson harpooning interlocking directorates and protecting 'business freedom', while Uncle Sam steers the boat.

'Le Poulpe colossal', after Denys de Montfort, from Henry Lee's book on octopuses, 1875.

the same thing to men in Mycenaean society. 'On the other hand', he sees fit to add,

> since it is conceivable that the artist-potters of the Mycenaean may have been women, we should not overlook possible symbolic significance for the female. Here, again, we must fall back upon present day psychoanalytic observation which reveals the extremely common unconscious wish in many women to have a penis just like a man.[5]

The octopus was commonly found on coins, gems, and ornaments from ancient Greece. Henry Lee records that the sixteenth-century Italian naturalist Ulisse Aldrovandi described the two coins used by the Syracusans, one of gold and one of bronze, as both having an octopus on one side. In his archaeological

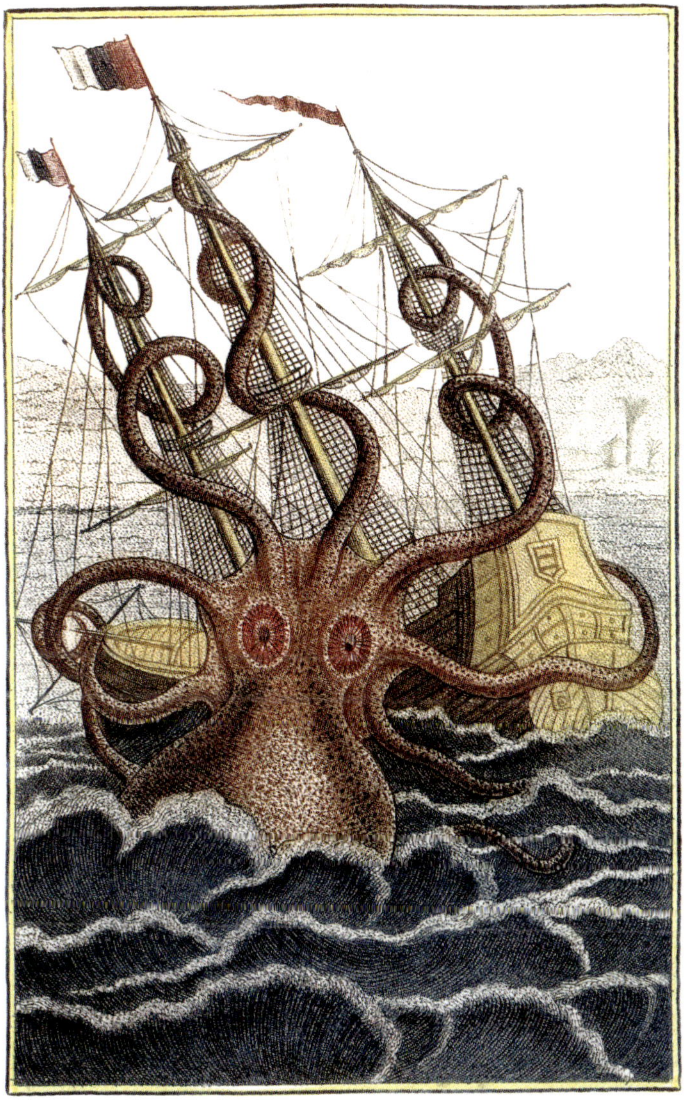

Greek vessel,
c. 1400 BCE.

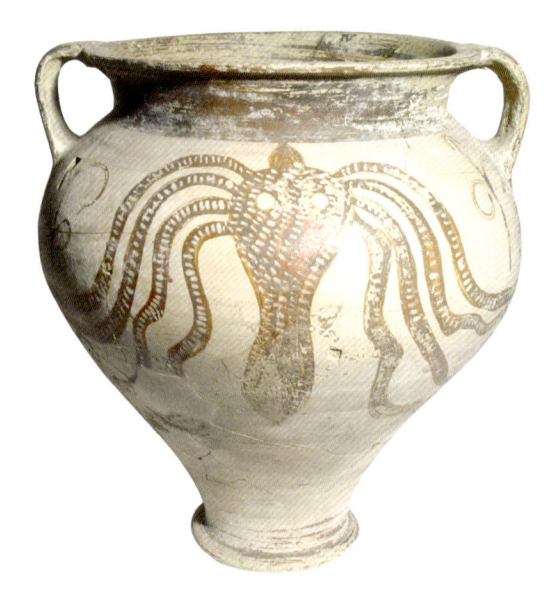

digs at Mycenae, beginning in 1876, Heinrich Schliemann revealed many octopus symbols. In one grave that he opened he found 53 small golden octopuses.[6] From its presence in the coin of the realm and also as something to accompany a dead body, it would seem that for these people the octopus might have represented prosperity rather than castration.

Whether or not the octopus was an archetypal symbol for the fear of castration among Mediterranean cultures is hard to say. It certainly does not appear to have had those connotations in first-century Pompeii, where it appears in a number of mosaics, including the mosaic of local marine life made with tiny tesserae, which has an octopus in the centre fighting with a lobster. It was found in one of Pompeii's most elegant homes, the House of the Faun, and is now in Naples's Museo Archeologico Nazionale.

Octopuses continued to appear occasionally down through the centuries, turning up as decoration in some odd places, such as a pillar of the eighteenth-century Saint-Sulpice church in Paris and the pedestal of the nineteenth-century statue of Neptune on Rome's Piazza Navona. Whether an octopus was a friend or foe, or neither, is often difficult to decipher. Is the octopus something to be feared or embraced? What is certain is that these are the two poles between which octopus iconography has alternated in the Western world, and they may not be as far apart as they seem.

An orgasm is not called a 'little death' for nothing. Pain and pleasure, as we all know, occur on a spectrum that changes depending on an individual's tastes. One person's brutal bestiality is another person's arousing transformation of an octopus into a lover. Some saw pleasure and others death in Hokusai's monumentally erotic

Octopús, ballet, with music composed by Labyala Nosfell and Pierre Le Bourgeois, 2010.

work, but what is certain is that by the end of the nineteenth century, many more Europeans were considering the image of the octopus than ever before.

What's more, they wanted to see one: to gaze on the real thing. While most people had never considered an octopus before Hugo's novel was published, subsequently everyone wanted a glimpse of one. Henry Lee, who spent many years at the public aquarium in Brighton, Sussex, wrote ten years after the books came out that thanks to Hugo's novel, an aquarium was now virtually required to have an octopus on exhibit if it wanted to draw the public.[7]

In East Asia, particularly in Japan, the octopus is more frequently thought of as a benevolent creature, although sometimes it is portrayed as slightly bumbling. But here, too, there is a cultural ambivalence towards the octopus. The tale on which Hokusai's woodblock was loosely based concerns an octopus that chases a brave young woman diver who is recovering a stolen jewel. The legend, the *Taishokan*, dates back to the Asuka period (538–710 CE) and its early versions portray the octopus as a

Kawanabe Kyōsai, woodblock print of a large rosary procession around an octopus, 1864.

monster fighting the girl for the jewel. Over the centuries, however, this changed. By the beginning of the Edo period (1603–1868), the diver had become increasingly sexualized, and the octopus more human. While some versions still portrayed the octopus attempting to overcome the diver by force, others began to suggest a sexual complicity between them.[8]

One Edo-period slang term for money was *o-ashi*, which means 'legs', perhaps because – then as now – there was nothing better to move you along than money. Things with many legs, such as cuttlefish and octopus, were considered auspicious gifts. The word *tako*, meaning octopus, during the Edo period was slang for vagina.[9]

A number of Buddhist temples feature octopuses, such as Kyoto's Tako Yakushi-do as well as Tako Yakushi hall at the Joju'in temple in the Meguro neighbourhood of Tokyo.[10] A rubbing stone from this temple is said to be good for curing warts, callouses, goitres and other types of protuberances.[11]

By the end of the Edo period the transformation of the octopus into an erotic object was complete. With the advent of photography, *shunga* became less popular as they were replaced by photographs of the real thing. Remarkably, in the digital age, octopuses are once again called on by Japanese culture to fulfil a role in the representation of explicit sex. Since the early 1960s, when the first pornographic films were shot and distributed in Japan, the government has banned films that show naked male and female genitalia. These days, despite the easy access to porn on the Internet in Japan, and its enormous popularity, penises are always blurred out. In a lot of Japanese pornography an octopus arm is a stand-in for a penis. This is done so frequently that an entire category of Japanese porn has developed which goes under the rubric of 'tentacle sex'. A Google search turns up thousands of sites where Web users can watch videos of Japanese women, often with their bodies oiled, being pleasured (or tortured, depending on the viewer's perception) by tentacles.

Tentacle erotica even has its own entry on Wikipedia.com:

> Tentacle erotica describes a type of pornography most commonly found in Japan. It integrates elements of traditional pornography with horror or science-fiction themes. Tentacle erotica can be of a consensual nature, but frequently has elements of non-consensual sex. Tentacle rape or *shokushu goukan* is found in some horror or *hentai* titles, with tentacled creatures (usually fictional monsters) having sexual intercourse with female characters.

Some sites feature videos of women being caressed and penetrated by tentacles made of plastic or hard rubber, but many of them feature animated tentacle sex. The cartoon women are standard; round-eyed, innocent-looking schoolgirls. Often they are repulsed and horrified by the tentacles that are violating them, but just as often their fear subsides into pleasure followed by ecstasy. These cartoons form part of the huge body of Japanese animated porn called *hentai*, loosely translatable as sexual weirdness. The women, whether real or cartoons, frequently have their hands tied to a bedstead, but despite their helplessness and the awful tentacles sliding all over their bodies and entering their orifices, their writhings, facial expressions and gasping moans leave no doubt that, like Hokusai's fisherman's wife, they are finding their experience an exquisite torture.

Utagawa Kuniyoshi, woodblock print showing octopuses demonstrating human pastimes and diversions, c. 1840–42.

The octopus is clearly still seen as an important bearer of pleasure in Japanese culture. In fact, pornography in present-day Japan is the primary source of sexual pleasure for many Japanese men. A full one-third of Japanese men between the ages of 20 and 30 do not want to bother with a sexual relationship, but

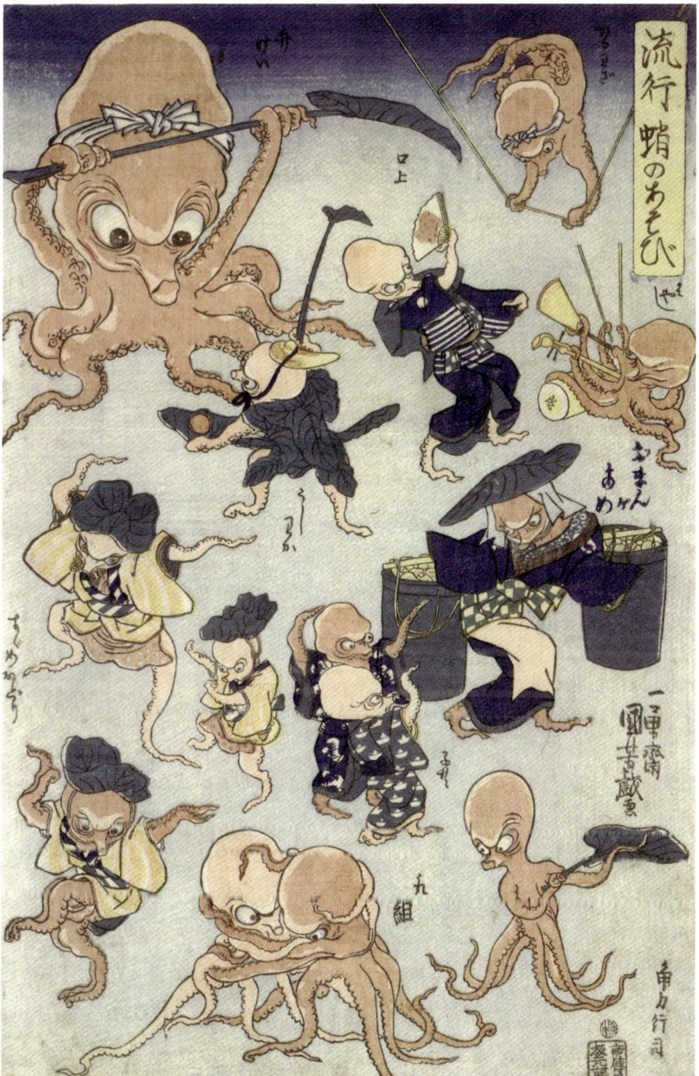
流行蛸のあそび
口上
九組
一勇斎國芳戯画

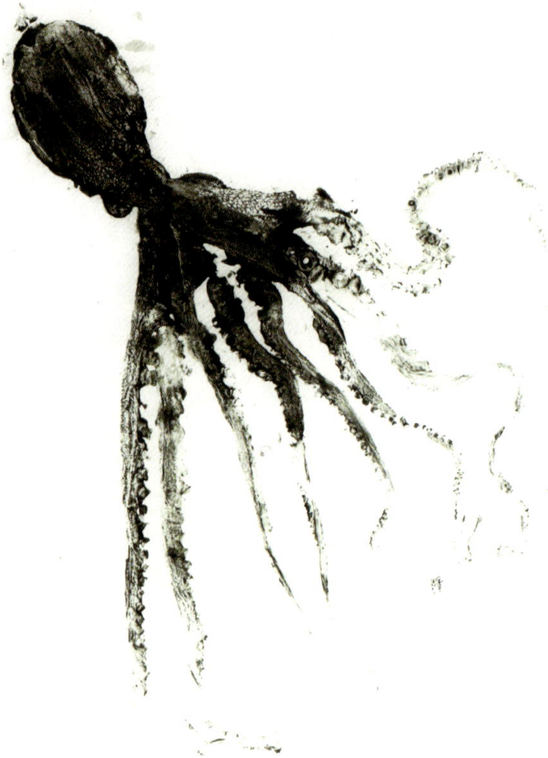

prefer to pay for the gratification of an orgasm, or do the job themselves utilizing pornography as a stimulant, according to French director Pierre Caule's documentary *L'Empire des sans* (*The Empire of Without*, 2010).

Tentacles can also be a woman's best friend, as Hokusai pointedly illustrated in 1814, and as the New York artist Zak Smith showed in 2005 with his series *100 Girls and 100 Octopuses*. Smith, whose work is often compared to that of Gustav Klimt, has acknowledged that the series is a homage to Hokusai. The 100 girls and octopuses are rendered in acrylics and metallic ink on paper, and each presents us with a woman and an octopus inside brightly coloured environments and patterns. In many of them the octopus is pleasuring the woman, and in others they are just keeping each other amicable company. The women are always young and often intriguing, a little strange, and unabashed in their enjoyment of their octopus companions. In an interview, Smith said:

> What I noticed is that the octopus usually comes up in the work of really stylish, stylized artists. Klimt, James Bond, Japanese woodblock art, *Gravity's Rainbow* – not only are there girls and octopuses in this stuff but also bizarre patterns and weird furniture and decadent carpets and lavish architecture. Octopuses tend to be the province of people who just wanna make gorgeous, crazy pictures, not sober, responsible artists who think their work will solve all the planet's problems or make them important.[12]

Klimt used the octopus in his painting *Jurisprudence* (1899–1907), which was later destroyed by the Nazis. In the painting a condemned man was depicted surrounded by the three female furies: Truth, Justice, and Law. They were shown as the Eumenides, the Greek deities of vengeance, punishing the condemned man,

Victòria Rabal, *gyotaku* of an octopus, 2011, Chinese ink on Japanese paper.

who was painted hunched and naked, wrapped in an octopus's arms. Anyone who has ever been involved in a lengthy court case will recognize the sensation of being surrounded on all sides.

Another visual artist who frequently creates octopuses is Miquel Barceló, Spain's most important contemporary painter. Barceló currently lives between Mali and Paris, but he was born and raised on the Mediterranean island of Majorca. In May 2011, in an interview with the newspaper *El País*, he said:

> I've hunted thousands [of octopuses], but now I don't kill them, and I scarcely eat them, because it's difficult to eat an animal to which you relate so much. Octopuses mean a lot to me. I watch them for hours. They're amazing. They have a memory, and their brains are capable of warehousing images. I'm trying to learn.[13]

Barceló's work frequently depicts octopuses. He was given a chapel in Majorca's huge, gothic cathedral La Seu to work with as he wished. What he did was wall the chapel, which dates back to 1229 CE, with a gigantic polychrome mural, taking the miracle of the loaves and fishes from the Gospel of John as a starting point. The creation, done between 2001 and 2007, includes numerous marine species, and octopuses turn up in more than one place. Barceló has said that he was attempting to create a sensation of being underwater, watching the live fish above the viewer's head. 'Heraclitus said it: "As above, so below"', he explained in the *El País* interview.

Unfortunately, few of those who use the visual image of an octopus do so with the respect and wonder that Zak Smith or Miguel Barceló bring to their work. Most tend to settle for the cheap thrill, the easy representation of *the other* as frightening and threatening. The website 'Vintage Octopus Pulp Covers' has collected some 90 examples of comic book covers that featured octopuses between the 1920s and 2002. They all portray the animal as menacing and evil.[14] And it's not just lowbrow literature that treats the octopus meanly: witness Thomas Pynchon's *Gravity's Rainbow* (1973), arguably one of the best books of the twentieth century by a North American author. One of its minor characters is an octopus with the 'gigantic, horror-movie devilfish name of Grigori', prepared by Pavlovian training to attack one of the book's heroines on a beach. A bad octopus, in other words.

The most famous and prolific of Hollywood's B-movie directors, Roger Corman, used a tentacle rape scene in his film *The Dunwich Horror* (1970). Things haven't changed much since then. A couple of fairly recent horror flicks, *Octopus* (2000) and *Octopus II: River of Fear* (2002), are typical: both portray a giant, mutated octopus attacking everything from submarines to buses.

The Struggle of the Slav, 1900: a Russian man fights an octopus labelled 'Bureaucracy' using an axe that reads 'Nat'l Assembly'.

Monster of the Abyss, a sci-fi underwater encounter, French.

In 1992 Roland Anderson published an article in *Of Sea and Shore* about octopuses in films. He wrote:

> Octopuses and squids, usually of the giant variety, have long figured prominently in movies. They are usually portrayed as 'monsters of the deep' with insatiable appetites for human flesh, reaching gigantic proportions, able to drag down ships or submarines with ease, and use hard hat or SCUBA divers for appetizers or dessert. They frequently have a propensity for lurking in sunken ships, particularly guarding the treasure chest of gold or pearls we know all sunken ships have on board.[15]

That image is not so different from the *Taishokan* legend in which an octopus struggles with a diver over a jewel, and which gave rise to Hokusai's woodblock. Anderson found about 60 films in which cephalopods made a significant appearance, including at least one that closely fits the *Taishokan* archetype. In a John Wayne film, *Wake of the Red Witch* (1948), the actor battles a giant octopus guarding a treasure of pearls, recovering them for their rightful owners.

Anderson found that only about 10 per cent of the films he reviewed featured a benevolent octopus, while the rest portrayed them as monsters. One film that bucks this current is Jean Painlevé's lyrical fourteen-minute documentary *The Love Life of an Octopus*, shot in 1965. Painlevé was a scientist, a pioneer in underwater film-making, a naturalist and a Surrealist. His documentary contains strikingly intimate footage of octopuses in all phases of life, from birth to copulation. We watch an octopus capture a crab and devour it: Painlevé somehow manages to have shot this from under the animal's mantle. We see a male initiate sex, couple and transfer his sperm. We are in a mother octopus's den as she uses her arms and jets of water to keep her strings of

Standard Oil as an octopus.

'War is Prussia's National Industry': German territories depicted as a land-grabbing octopus in a poster dating from the First World War.

eggs clean, and eventually we see them hatch. This remarkably close-up, detailed and beautiful look at the life of an octopus is all set to a lovely Surreal score by Pierre Henry.[16]

Unfortunately, this deep appreciation of the nuances of octopus life is the exception to the rule. Far more typical of how octopuses have been treated in film is the horror movie *It Came from Beneath the Sea* (1955), in which an octopus is mutated by an underwater H-bomb test and comes to terrorize the West Coast, ultimately destroying the Golden Gate Bridge. The film's heroes save the city by destroying the giant octopus with an atomic torpedo.

Most octopus-themed films have other things in common as well – low budgets, bad actors and perfunctory direction – but even when they form part of more impressive cinematic efforts, such as John Wayne's title or the James Bond film *Octopussy* (1983), they generally fall far short of communicating the wonder of the octopus. In *Octopussy* the indomitable 007 is pitted against an

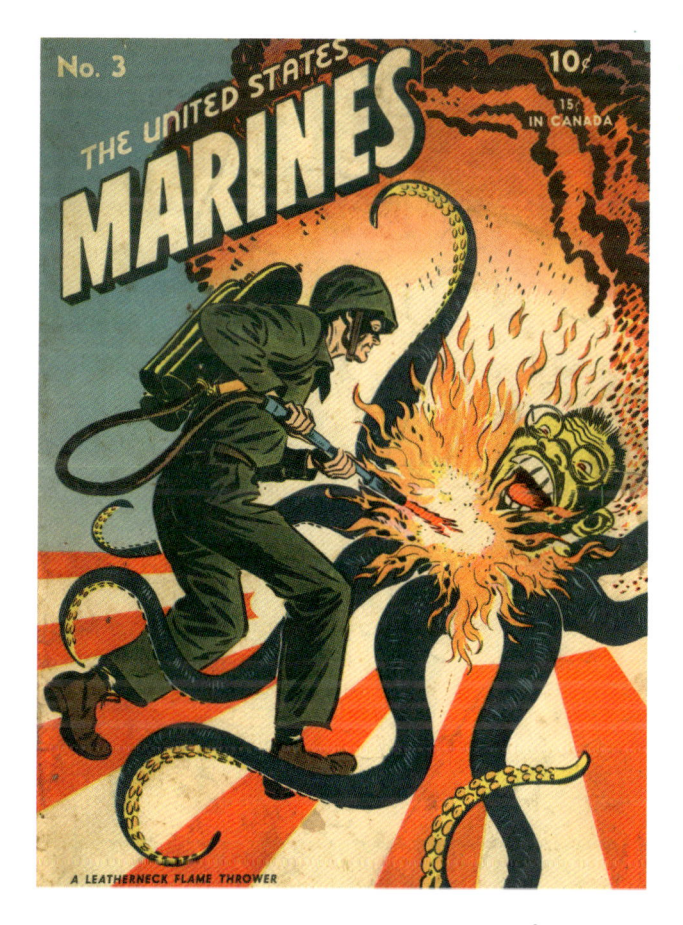

'A Leatherneck Flame Thrower' attacks the grasping, gasping enemy, c. 1944.

octopus cult of jewel-smuggling women, led by an octopus expert's daughter who keeps a deadly blue-ringed octopus as a pet. Here again is the connection between beautiful women, jewels and octopuses also found in *Taishokan*. Another box office success was Walt Disney's *20,000 Leagues under the Sea* (1954), which burned into the brains of a whole generation of adolescent

Captain Nemo observing a giant octopus.

moviegoers like myself the image of an evil giant squid wrapping the submarine *Nautilus* in its tentacles.

In 2002 the Disney conglomerate continued promoting the image of an evil octopus in its Peter Pan-based production *Return to Never Land*. In this film the evil crocodile in the original version of *Peter Pan* is replaced by an octopus, friend to the dastardly Captain Hook and enemy of the child heroes. More recently the studio continued its anti-octopus indoctrination of young children with *Jake and the Never Land Pirates*, an animated musical television show for children which first aired in February 2012 on the Disney Junior channel, and is also built around Disney's *Peter Pan* franchise machine.

The Disney Studios do not hold exclusive rights to octopus calumny on television, according to Anderson. Among the scant octopus appearances on the small screen, he notes an episode of *The Lucy Show* in 1964 which portrayed Lucille Ball having a nightmare in which she visits a haunted castle and encounters various monsters, including an octopus. A *Baywatch* episode from 1992 has the hunky men and women of the southern California lifeguard squad encountering a menacing giant octopus in an underwater grotto. It's not all bad. In an episode from September 1964 of the television series *The Addams Family*, based on the wonderful drawings of Charles Addams, the oldest son of Morticia and Gomez, Pugsley Uno Addams, causes his parents great concern when he joins the Boy Scouts and begins to like puppies better than his pet octopus Aristotle. Fortunately he's only going through a phase and his affection for the cephalopod returns.

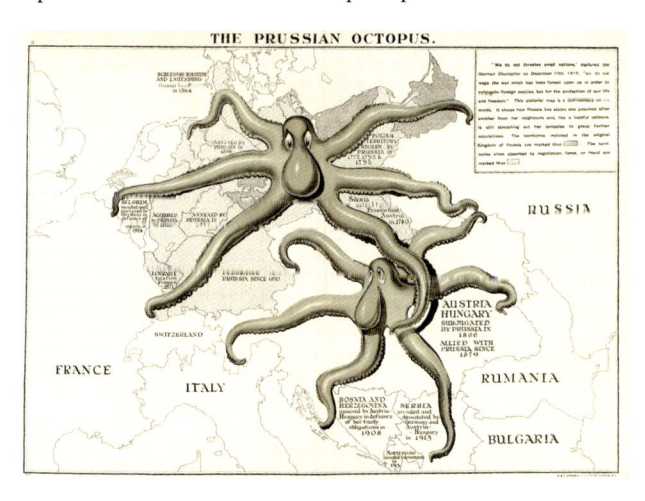

'The Prussian Octopus', poster showing Prussia and Austro-Hungary as invading octopuses, c. 1915.

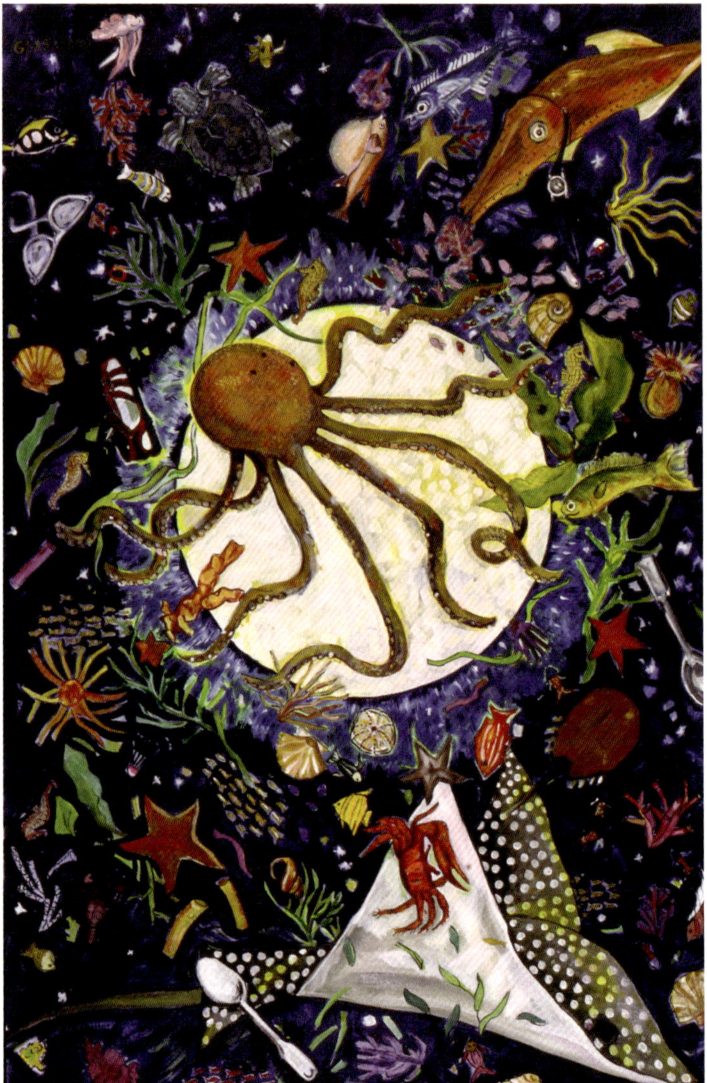

Paul the Octopus predicts that Spain will win the 2010 World Cup.

One octopus recently won the hearts of television viewers around the world. An *Octopus vulgaris* named Paul, and nicknamed the 'psychic octopus' by the popular press, was born at Weymouth, Dorset, on January 2008, and was acquired by the Sea Life Aquarium in Oberhausen, Germany. Paul showed a remarkable talent for predicting the results of European football matches. Two glass containers, each with a mussel inside, were placed in Paul's tank, each container representing a team, and he consistently picked the mussel out of the eventual winner's container. In 2010 he endeared himself to Spaniards, and amazed the rest of the world, by correctly predicting Spanish victories in the World Cup semi-finals and finals. The nation mourned when Paul began senescing and died in December of that year at the ripe old age of one year and eleven months.

Public perception of the octopus continues to swing from one extreme to the other, from Pablo Picasso to Walt Disney, and it

This cheerful painting of the sea's wonderful fauna by Donna Glassford, entitled *The Distance to the Moon*, hangs in the Vanderbilt University Children's Hospital in Nashville, Tennessee.

seems that there is no escaping this dichotomy. What is clear is that over the centuries the octopus has continued to both frighten and thrill us. Death and desire; bearer of pain and of pleasure; enemy and lover: an octopus is all these things to us, and always will be.

7 Octopus Keeping

> Reaction: bleeding for about 10 minutes; bee sting like with redness and local swelling. It lasted about 2 hours, still sore the next day.
> Roy Caldwell, description of an octopus bite[1]

An octopus is not designed to be a good pet. It is tremendously shy and retiring, and prefers a solitary life, lived apart even from other members of its own species, let alone human beings. It requires a lot of space in a well-kept saltwater aquarium. It rarely chooses to show itself, at least during the initial phase of its captivity. In addition, it is a genius at escaping, and will probably die a natural death in less than a year from its acquisition. Nevertheless people do keep them at home, and despite all these drawbacks an octopus can make a pleasant addition to a collection of marine animals. Apart from hobbyists, two other types of people routinely keep octopuses: those who manage public aquariums, and those doing scientific research.

No one who keeps an octopus will say it is easy to do. Much attention, care and expenditure are all required. Those charged with the maintenance and health of octopuses in public aquariums, and those who keep them in laboratory settings, are at least professionals who have the resources and the time to keep their octopuses happy. However, the third group of octopus-keepers, people with home aquariums, are likely to make some mistakes if they do not educate themselves first.

It is extremely important to know which species you are buying. Some species should not be kept in captivity because they are rare. This applies, for instance, to the 60-cm-long (2-foot)

Octopus maya bite.

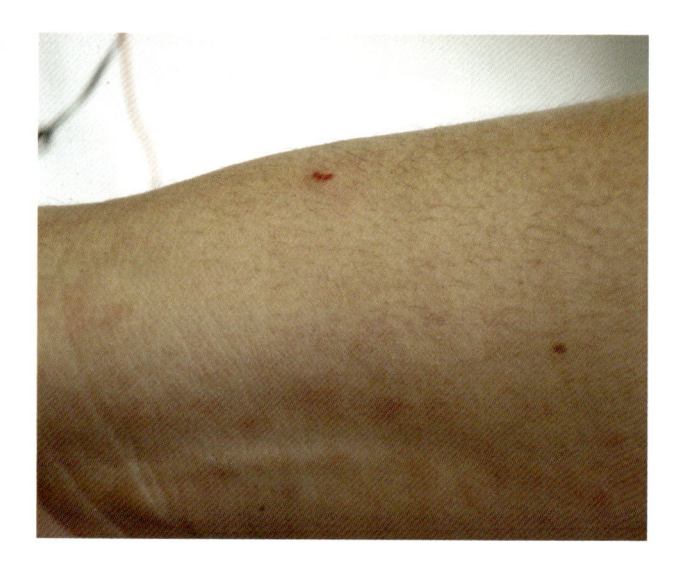

mimic octopus, *Thaumoctopus mimicus,* which lives only in the tropical seas of Malaysia and Indonesia, and was not officially discovered until 1998. It lives in flat, muddy areas of the bottom of the sea, and scientists speculate that it developed its mimicry capacity for defensive purposes, since it lacks a place to hide. It is able not only to camouflage itself in accordance with its surroundings, as many cephalopod species do, but to mimic other species physically and in its movements. It can transform its appearance into that of the poisonous sole fish, which is abundant where the mimic octopus lives, by drawing its arms together and undulating through the water like a flatfish, looking enough like a sole to discourage attacks. Another of the mimic's favourite strategies is to change to the ringed colours of the highly venomous sea snake and put six arms in a shallow hole while waving the two others separately, looking for all the world like a pair of sea snakes.[2]

In the first decade of the twenty-first century the popularity of mimic octupuses in home aquariums grew rapidly, so much so that some cephalopod experts began to get worried. In 2002 Roy Caldwell, a professor of integrative biology at the University of California, Berkeley, cautioned on a cephalopod website:

> If there is one thing that we know about mimics, it is that they are rare. Since they were first recognized, very few have been collected or observed in the wild. However, the habitats apparently suitable for the mimic are limited, easily accessible and the number of people (including collectors) diving on them is rapidly increasing ... I would urge everyone, amateurs and professionals alike, to curtail your desire to display these animals.[3]

Octopuses have remarkable camouflage abilities, but none more so than the mimic octopus.

According to experts, the first thing to do for those who want to keep an octopus, regardless of the species, is become adept at maintaining a saltwater aquarium. Any octopus needs to have at least a 190-litre (50-gallon) living space, and needs to have that space to itself. Any other living creature is likely to be viewed as prey.

It is best to learn how to maintain a saltwater aquarium at a time when the aquarium is occupied by marine fish with less exacting biological requirements than an octopus. Roland Anderson and Jennifer Mather, in their book *Octopus*, suggest the colourful damselfish.[4] The initial step, whatever species is to be kept, is obtaining a steady supply of salt water. Unpolluted fresh water can be transformed for the aquarium by adding sea salt, according to Anderson and Mather, which is available at pet shops. The water needs to have a pH of about 8.2. They recommend using up to three different types of filters to maintain water quality.[5] Time and money will need to be spent. Inside the aquarium, an octopus will need a good hiding place, a private space where it can retreat from view. It should never have to live somewhere without such an area.

However, merely providing an octopus with decent food and housing is not enough, say the experts. They also need to have their minds stimulated. A relatively new theory among researchers who work with captive animals, 'environmental enrichment', refers to the need to provide variation and interest in an animal's surroundings and daily life. Nancy King, who writes about keeping octopuses for the cephalopod-lovers' website www.tonmo.com, advises:

> Some octopuses like to play with toys. Most will play tug of war with a feeding stick and maybe even your hand. Others prefer a pile of shells to sort through, various

baby toys such as a string of plastic rings, toy building blocks, or a construction of drinking straws. Octo-keepers have taught their octopuses to open a jar or container with a crab inside, starting with the lid barely screwed on. The hand of its keeper is also a favourite toy for the octopus.[6]

In an article in *Diseases of Aquatic Organisms* Anderson and Mather point out that when an octopus has food and a mate provided in an environment with no predation pressure, it is no longer pursuing its normal activity by searching for these things. They write:

> We know that intelligent animals and social ones get bored . . . in a captive animal boredom is usually exhibited by destructive behaviour, which can be directed against its enclosure, against the contents of its enclosure or against itself, its tank mates or its keeper.[7]

Anderson recommends using toys that can be explored and examined; that have parts the octopus can move with its arms and suckers; and that have levers and gears linked to other movable parts.[8] Each octopus has its own personality, and owners can experiment with a variety of toys to see which their octopus prefers.

Once a potential octopus owner understands the mechanics of setting up and maintaining a saltwater aquarium, and has provided an appropriate environment, the octopus's future home needs to be escape-proofed. This is far from simple. Octopuses' suckers are tremendously powerful. They enable an octopus to go straight up a glass wall or pull apart a pump or filter. Because it has no skeleton, it can squeeze through openings apparently far too small to accommodate it. Aquariums must either be covered in something like screening or Astroturf that the octopus cannot get a purchase on, or have an immovable lid. All filters, pumps and valves in the tank must be well-anchored.

Some species of octopuses appear to be more inclined towards escape behaviour than others, although there is little doubt that given an opportunity, any confined species will make a break for it. In an informal survey published in 2004 James Wood and Roland Anderson concluded that the common octopus, *Octopus vulgaris*, and the giant Pacific octopus, *Enteroctopus dofleini*, are among the species most likely to attempt a dash for freedom, while the California two-spot *Octopus bimaculoides* is less inclined to do so.[9]

Henry Lee, the naturalist and director of the Brighton Aquarium in 1875, recounted:

> In the early days of the Institution, and before precautions were taken to avert such accidents, an octopus drew up, by night, the waste-valve of his tank, and let all the water run out of it thus, by his strength, like Samson at Gaza, bringing death upon himself and all his companions.[10]

Jacques Cousteau wrote about watching octopuses squeeze into small spaces:

> The whole operation seems contrary to the laws of nature; and we have concluded, only half-jokingly, that the larger an octopus is, the smaller the opening through which it can pass. It has a fantastic ability to stretch itself thin, like rubber; or lengthen its arms, one after the other; to flatten its body. Even its head changes shape, and the eyes can be moved obliquely.[11]

A wealth of octopus escape stories exist just about anywhere octopuses are kept. Again, Henry Lee was the first to publish his account:

> In May 1873, we had one at the Brighton Aquarium which used regularly every night to quit its tank, and make its way along the wall to another tank some distance from it, in which were some young lump-fishes. Day after day, one of these was missing, until, at last, the marauder was discovered. Many days elapsed, however, before he was detected, for after helping himself to, and devouring a young 'lump-sucker', he demurely returned before daylight to his own quarters.[12]

Frank Lane, in *Kingdom of the Octopus*, recounts a story told to him by one C. W. Coates of the New York Zoological Society. Coates recalled that a collector in Florida once shipped ten octopuses to New York, each in a cigar box.

> Quarter-inch holes were drilled in the boxes and they were tightly bound with fish-line before bring put in the shipping tank. The lines tightened in the water, and held the boxes so tightly shut that when they were tested afterwards with a screwdriver it was found impossible to pry up the lids as much as an eighth-inch. Yet every one of the octopuses escaped.[13]

Even the renowned Anton Dohrn originally underestimated octopus determination and agility when he built the aquarium at his marine research station in Naples. When he opened it, in 1905, he had an octopus and a lobster in the same tank, separated only by a glass wall. In no time at all the octopus had scaled it and made short work of the lobster. Dohrn took out the octopus and modified the tank, building a wall between the two halves so the octopus could not see the new lobster. Graziano Fiorito told me how, as Dohrn watched, the octopus clambered over the wall, lobster clearly on its mind. After that the octopuses were housed in separate tanks.[14]

Jerome Lettvin, a cognitive scientist and neurophysiologist at the Massachusetts Institute of Technology, gained new respect for the invertebrates while he was doing research one summer at the Stazione Anton Dohrn.

> I had a pet octopus when I was in Naples. He was a big one, a huge one. 'Juvenile Delinquent' is what I called him. My son Jonathan would play with him. We'd come into the lab in the morning and the octopus would be waiting for us. Jonathan would climb into the tank, and instantly there would be a tug of war, back and forth . . .
>
> I teased JD – he was a big octopus, he had a 5-foot spread of arms – I teased him by holding a fish down for him to grab, then pulling it back . . . The next morning I walk into the lab and JD is up on the edge of his 20-foot tank. I walk in and smack! . . . right in my face . . . he let out a huge squirt of water! He had been waiting for me to come in.

Not only waiting, but also practising.

> I turn around and there are splotches of water all around the region of where my head would be when I come in. The octopus had planned his revenge and he had been practicing ahead of time. That sounds like a ridiculous story, eh? Well, it isn't.[15]

Mask of octopus hunter, British Columbia.

One of the most common octopuses in home aquariums in the U.S. is *O. bimaculoides*, a small octopus also called the California two-spot or the bimac. It adjusts to captivity more easily than other species, and in fact bimacs have become so popular that they are now bred in captivity for the pet trade. Obtaining a bimac that was born in captivity frees the purchaser from the guilt of having caged an animal accustomed to life in the wild.

When kept well, under correct conditions, an *O. bimaculoides* will reward its owner with familiarity and trust. Once it comes to know its owner as a harmless, non-threatening, reliable source of food, it may well feel comfortable out in the open, and even allow itself to be handled. For many people, that would be the apogee of their relationship with their pet octopus – to be able to hold it, to touch it and, in turn, to let it sample them with all its octopus senses.

But they had better be careful, because octopuses bite. Their beaks can deliver a serious wound. This doesn't necessarily mean that people should avoid keeping octopuses as pets, or even that they should not handle them. It does, however, reinforce the rule that they should know which species they are acquiring. The most dangerous is a small brown octopus, *Hapalochlaena maculosa*, also called the blue-ringed octopus for the brilliant blue rings in its brown colouration that appear when it is disturbed. It is found in the wild in Australia's coastal waters and the eastern Indo-Pacific. It has also reputedly appeared for sale in the octopus markets of the world, online and in pet shops. Its venom is tetrodotoxin (TTX), one of the most potent natural venoms known. TTX is the same poison found in the puffer fish that every year kills brave and foolhardy Japanese diners who consume *fugu*, a delicacy chefs must be specially licensed to serve. One milligram of TTX can rapidly kill a grown man, according to Roy Caldwell at the University of California, Berkeley, and one diminutive blue-ringed octopus has enough of the venom to paralyse ten people.

Those who live for 24 hours after the bite are likely to recover. Symptoms normally begin shortly after being bitten. 'Within five to ten minutes, the victim begins to experience parasthesia and numbness, progressive muscular weakness and difficulty breathing and swallowing', writes Caldwell. 'Nausea and vomiting, visual disturbances and difficulty speaking may also occur. In severe cases, this is followed by flaccid paralysis and respiratory failure, leading to unconsciousness and death due to cerebral anoxia.'[16]

Fortunately *H. maculosa* is the only octopus species endowed with such a toxic venom. The rest of the octopuses in the world will deliver a bite that is not mortal, and in most cases not even very debilitating, but which is nonetheless unpleasant. A person's reaction to an octopus bite depends on both the species of octopus doing the biting, and the constitution of the person who is bitten. An octopus bite is rather like a bee sting, and ranges in size from a tiny, two-point puncture to a small wound. Like a bee sting, it can be quite painful, and some people will be more sensitive to its effects than others.

Researchers at the University of Melbourne are examining the structure of cephalopod venom and how it works. Lead investigator Brian Fry has said that all octopuses carry some amount of toxic proteins, which they mix with saliva to paralyse their prey.[17] The goal of his research is to decipher cephalopod toxins and apply his findings to drugs for humans. While all octopuses have some level of poison mixed with their saliva, the

The blue-ringed octopus can kill an adult human with one bite.

molecular composition of the venoms changes with the species. One strong candidate for pharmaceutical use is the venom of a small Mediterranean octopus, *Eledone moschata*. It forms a protein called eledoisin in its venom gland, which also has strong vasodilating (blood vessel-widening) properties.[18]

In addition to the venom it injects along with its saliva, octopus ink is also toxic. It too has aroused interest in its potential pharmacological properties. If an adult octopus inks in an aquarium, it may suffocate itself, as the dense ink will cover the creature's gills, but recent research seems to show that in addition

Toyota Hokkei, woodblock print of a catch including an octopus and a puffer fish, c. 1818–30.

Poster for the film *It Came from Beneath the Sea* (1955).

to its density and its ability to momentarily hide a fleeing octopus, cephalopod ink could function as a weapon. It has been shown to be toxic to some cells, and actually to kill certain kinds of tumour cells.[19]

Jacques Cousteau had serious doubts about whether octopuses bite, writing that he had never seen it happen.[20] Octopus researcher Martin J. Wells, on the other hand, had no doubts at all:

> People are occasionally bitten by *Octopus vulgaris*. I have been bitten ten or twenty times myself and nearly all of the research workers that I know, working regularly with this species, have been bitten at one time or another, normally while carrying the animals between aquaria ... The beaks are comparatively blunt and in the majority of cases it is unlikely that saliva is injected.[21]

A contented octopus is probably less likely to bite, so it's important to keep a captive octopus well fed. Adults are generally fed frozen seafood, and a lot of it. That's okay if a person lives near the coast, but inlanders can wind up paying quite a bit for their octopus's diet. At any rate, uniformity in feeding hours is recommended. In some cases feeding time will be the only time of the day when an octopus will allow itself to be seen. Creating the correct kind of complex environment with plenty of places to hide and the occasional toy with which to play will also contribute to an octopus's sense of well-being.

A contented octopus is obviously also going to cooperate more readily in a public aquarium or a research lab. And an octopus with a grudge, or just with too much time on its hands and too little to occupy its attention, can do a lot of damage, wreak a lot of havoc and make a lot of mischief. In 2009, at the Santa Monica Pier Aquarium, a small California two-spot octopus swam to the top of its tank one night, after everyone had closed up and gone home, and took apart the valve controlling the recycling system. Some 200 gallons of seawater spilled out before the first employee entered the room ten hours later. The *Los Angeles Times* reported that no harm was done to either the aquarium or the octopus. That was not the case, however, in 2004, when a giant Pacific octopus at the Cabrillo Marine Aquarium in San Pedro, California, took apart the plastic tubing that formed part of the tank's drain, and let all the water out of its tank, only to be found dead the next morning in a dry tank.[22]

Aquariums are the only locations where most people will ever see an octopus, and even then they are not likely to see much of them. However, the American actor Mark Wahlberg's son saw too much of one of them. The toddler had a nasty run-in with a giant Pacific octopus, according to the actor, who was quoted on a celebrity website in 2010:

We have a tour guide so she's like, 'You have a special treat today, we'll be able to take you behind the tank and you'll be able to see the octopus' . . . So this woman pulls out this gigantic octopus, the thing latches on to my son's arm. It's got my wife, [it's] wrapped completely around the lady, and another guy's just standing there. They can't get this octopus off. My son is freaking out but no sound is coming out of his mouth. So finally we rip the thing off of him. He's got all these suction marks that look like about 30 little hickeys [love-bites] . . . He [the aquarium manager] said it's never been that aggressive.[23]

An *Octopus vulgaris* in the Barcelona Aquarium.

The only humans to have regular contact with octopuses, other than octopus fishermen, pet owners and public aquarium employees, are researchers and lab technicians. In 1991 the UK's Universities Federation for Animal Welfare published a handbook on the care and management of cephalopods in the laboratory, written by marine biologist Peter Boyle. He noted:

> In the laboratory, numerous experimental studies have described remarkable capabilities of sensory discrimination, especially of visual stimuli; they have demonstrated that true learning occurs and is likely to be an integral aspect of the normal life of an octopus. These qualities of behavioural complexity, sensory discrimination and learning in cephalopods bear comparison with those of many lower vertebrates and provide ample cause for con-

Gloria Bornstein, sculpture of an octopus in the Neototems Children's Garden at the Seattle Center.

A late 19th-century Czech watercolour of *Octopus macropus*, the Atlantic white-spotted octopus.

sidering their welfare in the laboratory for humane and scientific reasons.[24]

Boyle's recommendations are just that in most places where octopuses are kept: recommendations. His homeland, the UK, has some regulations which apply only to octopuses. Canada also regulates cephalopod research, although its giant neighbour to the south does not have any regulations regarding invertebrate research. Researchers in European Union countries have had no choice about the basic level of care they must afford their captive cephalopods from January 2013 onwards. An EU directive passed in November 2010 stipulated that as of 2013 cephalopod research subjects must be treated exactly the same as mammalian subjects like monkeys or mice. This means that those who are designing experiments with octopuses will need to have their work authorized by the national 'competent authority' responsible for the implementation of the directive. To gain approval, a project will have to provide information that includes the relevance of the research for which the cephalopods are to be used; details of housing and the conditions under which the animal will be cared for; the planned use of anaesthesia and analgesia to reduce pain; the ways in which an animal's suffering will be reduced to a minimum; how the animals will be sacrificed, if need be; and the qualifications of the project's personnel.

'The greatest concern for cephalopod researchers is an article in the directive that states that "animals taken from the wild shall not be used in procedures"', wrote Nicola Nosengo in an article about the legislation for *Nature*.[25] 'Exceptions will have to be justified, and the capture of animals in the wild should be carried out by "competent persons using methods which do not cause the animals avoidable pain, suffering, distress or lasting harm".'

Numerous researchers called for such standards well ahead of the EU. In 2007 an international group of cephalopod researchers – including scientists from Australia, South Africa, Europe, Japan, Brazil and the U.S. – published an article in the journal *Reviews in Fish Biology and Fisheries*. They wrote:

> When considering the welfare of vertebrate animals in experiments it is recommended that the three Rs (reduction, replacement, and refinement) be considered. This

involves ensuring that the number of animals used in the experiments is valid (reduction), considering alternatives to live animals in experiments (replacement), and adoption of experimental methods that minimize distress to the animals (refinement). We recommend that the three Rs should be a major consideration when using cephalopods in experiments.[26]

I can certainly agree with that. One gaze from an octopus is enough to convince a person that an intelligent, conscious being is behind that look, and it happened to me on a fishing boat off the Mediterranean coast. A newly captured octopus was loose on the deck. It was making its way around the aluminium surface, moving in an odd kind of dignified, hunched slither, with one of its eight arms extended in front of it, feeling around this completely new, out-of-water world like a blind person with a cane, processing information as it explored, searching for a way back to the sea, or a place to hide. It had turned a ruddy reddish-brown, which in octopus-speak was a clear sign that it was feeling threatened and was angry. I reached down, thinking to heft it up by one of its eight arms. It was slippery to the touch, virtually impossible to grip, and the arm flowed right through my hand. The octopus had no problem gripping me, however, and laid the sucker discs of another arm on the back of my groping hand to smell me, taste me, sense me — it was like being sniffed by an inquisitive dog.

At the same time, its glance met mine, and I gazed into its two pop eyes for an instant. I sensed a tightly-controlled panic, an urgent desperation, but I also saw something more than that. I was jolted by a sense of an individual behind those eyes, a thinking entity. I have pulled thousands of fish out of the water in my lifetime, but the look in this octopus's eye was something else

Sculpture of an octopus at Roanoke Island Aquarium, North Carolina.

entirely. Some sort of visual communication was going on between us, although it didn't last long. The octopus had no time for me. It flowed away to resume its fruitless investigations of the escape-proof boat, leaving faint, round love-bites on my skin where the suction discs had pulled my blood to the surface. The slipperiness left on my hand smelled of the sea – marine, but not fishy.

Neither the bruises nor the odour lasted long: they both disappeared from my skin before the boat got back to the dock. However, the memory of that gaze endured – the curious, disturbing and exciting sense of a mind behind those eyes. It is no easier for me to imagine what kind of mind that might be, than it would be for the octopus to understand what it is like to be inside my head. What octopus consciousness consists of is beyond my ken, but it is clearly a good idea to treat the animal with the highest respect when we're experimenting on it, setting catch limits for it or cooking it.

Invertebrates have often been regarded as nothing more than reproductive agglomerations of cells in occasionally edible flesh formations, animals with little mental life apart from the most basic and simple functions: living and dying; consuming and being consumed as part of a long food chain; excreting; and reproducing. However, the sophisticated neurology of the octopus's brain implies that an intelligence might flourish there, and its behaviour intimates a mind at work, although one quite different from that found in vertebrates.

Just remember: when you watch an octopus, an octopus watches you back.

Timeline of the Octopus

420 million years ago	350 million years ago	300 million years ago	200 million years ago
At the end of the Silurian period, cephalopods have relatively easy lives. They have shells and live close to the coasts	Fossils of long-extinct cephalopods are believed to date back this far, and are some of the oldest fossils on record	Piscine species become more abundant and with more sophisticated hunting skills than ever before. Octopuses, threatened, begin to internalize and eliminate their shells, and move to deeper waters	Octopuses have moved to deeper water and developed defensive alternatives such as camouflage and expelling ink

200 CE	538–710 CE	1324	1814
Claudius Aelianus, who writes *De natura animalium*, says of the octopus: 'Mischief and craft are plainly seen to be the characteristics of this creature'	The Japanese legend *Taishokan* portrays the octopus as a monster fighting a young, beautiful girl for a jewel. In later versions the octopus helps the girl, and some retellings even have the animal becoming her lover	The medieval Catalonian cookbook *Llibre de Sent Soví* has a recipe for preparing baked octopus, one of the first-known printed recipes in Europe for preparing octopus	Katsushika Hokusai produces his supremely erotic Japansese *shunga* woodblock print, known as *The Dream of the Fisherman's Wife*

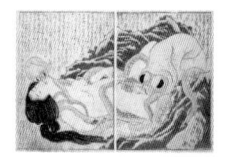

1928	1992	1993
John Z. Young, a British neurophysiologist, comes to the Stazione Zoologica Anton Dohrn on a scholarship from Oxford University and begins a lifetime of studying octopuses, eventually publishing *The Anatomy of the Nervous System of 'Octopus vulgaris'* in 1971	The world of octopus research is shaken to the core when *Science* publishes an article by an Italian neurobiologist, Graziano Fiorito, reporting that octopuses are capable of observational learning	Jennifer Mather, a professor of psychology and neuroscience from the University of Lethbridge in Alberta, Canada, teams up with Roland Anderson, director of the Seattle Aquarium, for the first of many interesting research projects into octopus consciousness

2000–1000 BCE

Pottery from the Middle and Late Minoan periods often features images of octopuses

500 BCE

The Greek poet Theognis of Megara writes of the octopus's amazing ability to change colours and blend in with its surroundings

350 BCE

Aristotle, in his *Historium animalium*, describes the octopus with great precision, erring only in concluding that the animal is 'stupid'

323 BCE

The Greek philosopher Diogenes dies at Corinth, possibly of colic after eating a raw octopus, or by a bite from a dog for which he was dividing an octopus

1866

Victor Hugo writes his immensely popular novel *Les Travailleurs de la mer* (*The Toilers of the Sea*), in which the octopus is portrayed as mankind's enemy. Gustave Doré's chilling illustrations for it become a popular image of the octopus as an implacable foe

1873

The Stazione Zoologica Anton Dohrn, a 19th-century building on the shore of the Bay of Naples, is inaugurated. It becomes the world's leading octopus research institute

1875

Henry Lee, a naturalist and director of the Brighton Aquarium, writes *The Octopus*, the first closely observed natural history of the animal, for general readers, in modern times

1910

A Frenchman from the Sorbonne, Henri Piéron, shows at the Stazione Zoologica Anton Dohrn that an octopus can learn to take a cork out of a jar to reach a crab inside it

2002

The Moroccan octopus catch in the Atlantic begins to decline and to follow the path of the Spanish catch, which went into decline in 1971 and never recovered

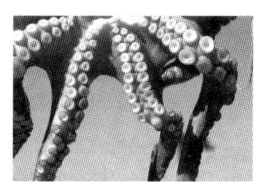

2005

New York artist Zak Smith completes his series of striking paintings, *100 Girls and 100 Octopuses*

2007

Spanish artist Miquel Barceló finishes his four-year project to construct a ceramic wall for a chapel in La Seu Cathedral, Palma, Majorca. Octopuses are a central presence in the work, depicting the miracle of the loaves and fishes from the Gospel of John

References

1 OCTOPUS BODY

1 Jacques-Yves Cousteau and Philippe Diolé, *Octopus and Squid: The Soft Intelligence* (New York, 1973), p. 88.
2 Roger T. Hanlon and John B. Messenger, *Cephalopod Behaviour* (Cambridge, 1996) p. 1.
3 M. J. Wells, *Octopus: Physiology and Behaviour of an Advanced Invertebrate* (London, 1978), p. 169.
4 Henry Lee, *The Octopus; or, the 'Devil-fish' of Fiction and of Fact* (London, 1875), p. xiv.
5 Frank W. Lane, *Kingdom of the Octopus* (New York, 1960), p. 1.
6 Wells, *Octopus*, p. 8.
7 Lee, *The Octopus*, pp. 29–30.
8 Quoted in Jennifer Tzar and Eric Scigliano, 'Through the Eyes of an Octopus', *Discover*, 24 (2003), p. 10.
9 Aristotle, *Historia animalium*, trans. D'Arcy Wentworth Thompson, Book IX, Part 37 (Oxford, 1910).
10 Martin Moynihan, *Communication and Noncommunication in Cephalopods* (Bloomington, IN, 1985), p. 95.
11 Wells, *Octopus*, p. 3.
12 Aristotle, *Historia animalium*, Book V, Part 6.
13 Jerome Wodinsky, 'Hormonal Inhibition of Feeding and Death in Octopus: Control by Optic Gland Secretion', *Science*, 198 (8 December 1977), pp. 948–51.
14 Lane, *Kingdom of the Octopus*, p. 50.
15 Ibid., p. 44.
16 Ibid., p. 173.

17 Hanlon and Messenger, *Cephalopod Behaviour*, p. 85.
18 'Novel Design Principles and Technologies for a New Generation of High Dexterity Soft-bodied Robots Inspired by the Morphology and Behavior of the Octopus', www.octopus-project.eu, 30 April 2009.
19 Wells, *Octopus*, pp. 225–7.
20 Ibid., p. 222.
21 Ibid., p. 209.
22 Lee, *The Octopus*, p. 24.
23 'Scientists Tap into Antarctic Octopus Venom', www.sciencedaily.com, 28 July 2010.
24 Jerome Wodinsky, 'Penetration of Shell and Feeding on Gastropods by Octopus', *American Zoologist*, 9 (1969), pp. 997–1010.
25 Jennifer Mather, 'Daytime Activity of Juvenile *Octopus vulgaris* in Bermuda', *Malacologia*, 29 (1988), pp. 69–76.
26 Jennifer A. Mather, Roland C. Anderson and James B. Wood, *Octopus: The Ocean's Intelligent Invertebrate* (Portland, OR, 2010), pp. 57–8.

2 OCTOPUS BRAIN

1 Aristotle, *Historia animalium*, trans. D'Arcy Wentworth Thompson, Book IX, Part 37 (Oxford, 1910).
2 Ted Bullock, quoted in 'What is this Octopus Thinking?', at www.scoopit.co.nz, accessed 24 October 2012.
3 Irmgard Müller, *The Naples Zoological Station at the Time of Anton Dohrn* (Naples, 1975), pp. 11–18.
4 Binyamin Hochner, Tal Shomrat and Graziano Fiorito, 'The Octopus: A Model for a Comparative Analysis of the Evolution of Learning and Memory Mechanisms', *The Biological Bulletin*, 210 (June 2006), pp. 308–17.
5 Ibid.
6 J. von Uexküll, *Leitfaden in das Studium der Experimentellen Biologie der Wassertierre* (Wiesbaden, 1905).

7 Henri Piéron, 'Contribution à la psychologie du poulpe: L'Acquisition d'habitudes', *Bulletin de l'Institut Général Psychologique* (14 November 1910), pp. 111–19.
8 F.J.J. Buytendjik, 'Das Verhalten von Octopus nach tielweiser Zerstörung des "Gehirns"', *Archives Néerlandaises des Sciences Exactes et Naturelles*, 3c/18 (1933), pp. 24–70.
9 Paul Schiller, 'Delayed Detour Response in the Octopus', *Journal of Comparative and Physiological Psychology*, XLII/3 (June 1949), pp. 220–25.
10 B. B. Boycott, *The History of Neuroscience in Autobiography*, ed. Larry R. Squire (San Diego, CA, 2001), vol. III, p. 52.
11 Ibid., pp. 52–5.
12 Ibid., p. 56.
13 Martin J. Wells, *Octopus: Physiology and Behaviour of an Advanced Invertebrate* (London, 1978), p. 224.
14 John Z. Young, *The History of Neuroscience in Autobiography*, ed. Larry R. Squire (San Diego, CA, 2001), vol. I, pp. 578–9.
15 Ibid., p. 583.
16 Bernardino Fantini, *The History of the Stazione Zoologica, Naples* (Naples, 2002), pp. 36–7.
17 James E. Barrett, 'Behavioral Determinant of Drug Action: The Contributions of Peter B. Dews', *Journal of the Experimental Analysis of Behavior*, LXXXVI/3 (November 2006), pp. 359–70.
18 P. B. Dews, 'Some Observations on an Operant in the Octopus', *Journal of the Experimental Analysis of Behavior*, 2 (January 1959) pp. 56–63.
19 Ibid., p. 62.
20 J. A. Mather, 'To Boldly Go Where No Mollusc has Gone Before: Personality, Play, Thinking, and Consciousness in Cephalopods', *American Malacological Bulletin*, 24 (2008), pp. 51–8.

3 OCTOPUS MIND

1 Graziano Fiorito and Pietro Scotto, 'Observational Learning in *Octopus vulgaris*', *Science*, 256 (24 April 1992), pp. 545–7.

2 Graziano Fiorito, interview with the author, May 2010.
3 Ibid.
4 Gerald B. Biederman, 'Social Learning in Invertebrates', *Science*, 259 (12 March 1993), pp. 1627–8.
5 Fiorito, interview with the author.
6 P. N. Dilly, 'Delayed Responses in Octopus', *Journal of Experimental Biology*, 40 (1963), pp. 393–440.
7 M. E. Bitterman, *Invertebrate Learning*, ed. William C. Corning (New York, 1975), vol. III, pp. 139–45.
8 Jennifer Mather, Roland Anderson and James B. Wood, *Octopus: The Ocean's Intelligent Invertebrate* (Portland, OR, 2010).
9 David Livingston Smith, interview with Jennifer Mather, *La ciudad de las ideas*, Part 1, available at www.youtube.com, April 2009.
10 Roland Anderson and Jennifer Mather, 'Octopuses are Smart Suckers!?', www.thecephalopodpage.org, accessed 24 October 2012.
11 Jennifer A. Mather and Roland C. Anderson, 'Personalities of Octopuses (*Octopus rubescens*)', *Journal of Comparative Psychology*, 107 (1993), pp. 336–40.
12 Jennifer A. Mather and Roland C. Anderson, 'Exploration, Play, and Habituation in *Octopus dofleini*', *Journal of Comparative Psychology*, 113 (1999), pp. 333–8.
13 Livingston Smith, interview with Jennifer Mather, Part 1.
14 Jennifer A. Mather, 'To Boldly Go Where No Mollusc Has Gone Before: Personality, Play, Thinking and Consciousness in Cephalopods', *American Malocological Bulletin*, 234 (2008), pp. 51–8.
15 Livingston Smith, interview with Jennifer Mather, Part 2.
16 Jean Boal, quoted in Michael Stroh, 'In the Lab it's Octopus See, Octopus Do – Behaviour Research', *Science News* (25 April 1992).
17 Garry Hamilton, 'What is this Octopus Thinking?', *New Scientist* (7 June 1997), p. 30.
18 Christelle Alves, Jean G. Boal and Ludovic Dickel, 'Short-distance Navigation in Cephalopods: A Review and Synthesis', *Cognitive Processing*, IX/4 (2008), pp. 239–47.

19 Jennifer A. Mather, 'Navigation by Spatial Memory and Use of Visual Landmarks in Octopuses', *Journal of Comparative Physiology A*, 168 (1991), pp. 491–7.
20 Mather and Anderson, 'Octopuses are Smart Suckers!?'
21 Gisella Kaufmann, 'Spineless Smarts: Interview with Jean Boal', www.pbs.org, July 2005.
22 Benyamin Hochner, 'A. The Octopus as a Model for a Successful Control of Movements in Flexible Arms; B. Evolutionary Approach to the Exploration of the Neural Basis of Learning and Memory', The Octopus Group, www.octopus.huji.ac.il, accessed 24 October 2012.

4 OCTOPUS FISHING, FARMING AND MARKETING

1 FAO Fisheries and Agriculture, Species Fact Sheets, '*Octopus vulgaris*', www.fao.org/fishery, accessed 24 October 2012.
2 Monterey Bay Aquarium, 'Seafood Watch', www.montereybayaquarium.org, accessed 24 October 2012.
3 Pedro F. Seixas and Manuel Rey-Méndez, 'Potential Use of Octopus Species for Aquaculture: Present State of the Situation, Perspectives and Limitations', paper given at 'Aqua 2006', Florence, Italy, at www.was.org, accessed 24 October 2012.
4 Eileen Byrne, 'Sardines and Sovereignty in Western Sahara', *Congressional Record* (22 July 2004), p. 17275.
5 Fishery Resources Monitoring System Fact Sheet, 'Octopus – Morocco, Dakhla Zone, 2006', http://firms.fao.org, accessed 14 June 2013.
6 '2009 Report of the Working Group on Cephalopod Fisheries and Life History (WGCEPH)', www.ices.dk, accessed 24 October 2012.
7 Bruce Sundquist, 'Fishery Degradation: A Global Perspective – Chapter 5, Harvest and Population Data by Species', October 2009, http://home.windstream.net/bsundquist1.
8 FAO Fisheries and Agriculture, '*Octopus vulgaris*'.
9 N. Yagi, M. Ariji, A. Takahara and Y. Senda, 'Application of a Bioeconomics Model to Examine Sustainability of Fishery

Resources in the Global Market: The Case of Octopus Resource in Morocco', *Fisheries Science*, LXXV/1, pp. 43–6.
10 'Blue Ocean Institute – Seafood – Octopus', www.blueocean.org, accessed 14 June 2013.
11 '60 Injured after Moroccan-Sahrawi Clashes in Dakhla', www.afrol.com, 23 July 2008.
12 Gilbert L. Voss and Manuel Solis Ramírez, '*Octopus maya*, A New Species from the Bay of Campeche, Mexico', *Bulletin of Marine Science*, XVI/3 (1966), pp. 616–25.
13 '12 mil tons de pulpo esto año', http://holayucatan.com.mx, 27 July 2011.
14 Instituto Nacional de la Pesca, 'Evaluacion de la población de pulpo (*Octopus maya*) en la península de Yucatán 2007', www.inapesca.gob.mx, July 2007.
15 'El pulpo alcanza un precio récord de $105 por kilo: Enorme derrama económica en Progreso', www.progresohoy.com, 20 December 2011.
16 Aristotle, *Historia Animalium*, trans. D'Arcy Wentworth Thompson (Oxford, 1910), Book IV.
17 Oppian, *Halieutica*, trans. A. W. Mair (Chicago, IL, 1928), p. 425.
18 Richard Schweid, 'Armed and Delicious', *Departures* (July–August 2007), p. 135.
19 Alexis Tsangridis, Pilar Sanchez and Despina Ionnidou, 'Exploitation Patterns of *Octopus vulgaris* in Two Mediterranean Areas', *Scientia Marina*, LXVI/1 (2002), pp. 59–68.
20 'Seafood Watch Seafood Report: Tako (Madako), Common Octopus, *Octopus vulgaris*', www.montereybayaquarium.org, 20 August 2008.
21 '*Takoyaki* of Osaka – Mecca del Takoyaki (Octopus Balls)', www.geocities.jp/general_sasaki/takoyaki, accessed 24 October 2012.
22 K. Itami, Y. Izawa, S. Maeda and K. Nakai, 'Notes on the Laboratory Culture of the Octopus Larvae', *Bulletin of the Japanese Society of Scientific Fisheries*, XXIX/6 (1963), pp. 514–19.
23 J. Iglesias et al., 'Rearing of *Octopus vulgaris* Paralarvae: Present Status, Bottlenecks and Trends', *Aquaculture*, 266 (2007), pp. 1–15.

24 'Rinde frutos la primera granja de pulpo en el mundo', *Revista Yucatán*, 15 November 2009.
25 Carlos Rosas Vázquez, interview with the author, March 2010.
26 'Yucatán: Consume incendio primera granja de pulpos en el mundo', www.sipse.com, accessed 24 October 2012.
27 Vincent Cutrone, interview with the author, February 2007.

5 OCTOPUS CUISINE

1 Luís Gallego, interview with the author, January 2007.
2 Andrew Dalby, *Food in the Ancient World: From A to Z* (London, 2003), p. 22.
3 Ibid., p. 236.
4 Paul Bartsch, 'Pirates of the Deep: Stories of the Squid and Octopus', *Smithsonian Institute Annual Report for 1916*, pp. 347–75.
5 Diogenes Laërtius, *Lives of Eminent Philosophers*, trans. Robert Drew Hicks (Cambridge, MA, 1925), vol. II, Athenaeus, 8.341.
6 Pliny the Elder, *Natural History*, 10:133.
7 *Apicius*, Book IX:5.
8 'San Salvio, Martír', www.eltestigofiel.org, accessed 24 October 2012.
9 Anonymous, *Llibro de Sent Soví: El Primer Recetario Medieval de la Cocina Española* (Barcelona, 2008), p. 111.
10 J. Antonio Fidalgo Santamariña, *La gran pulpada gallega: Consideraciones historico-antropológicas sobre la fiesta del pulpo de Carballiño* (Barcelona, 1999).
11 Henry Lee, *The Octopus; or, The 'Devil-fish' of Fiction and of Fact* (London, 1875), pp. 84–5.
12 'Takoyaki Wars Shift to Tokyo', www.japantimes.co.jp, 1 April 2001.
13 'Unagi, Uni, Squid, Octopus Balls, Anglerfish and Seafood in Japan', http://factsanddetails.com/japan, accessed 24 October 2012.
14 Alan Davidson, 'Octopus', at www.huffingtonpost.com/encyclopedia/definition, accessed 24 October 2012.
15 Dalby, *Food in the Ancient World*, p. 236.
16 Vincent Cutrone, interview with the author, February 2007.

17 Jason Kessler, 'The Octopus is Ready for Its Closeup', www.foodrepublic.com, 8 March 2008.
18 Vincent Cutrone, interview with the author, February 2007.
19 Lee, *The Octopus*, pp. 88–9.
20 Eric Ripert, interview with the author, February 2007.

6 OCTOPUS ICONOGRAPHY

The epigram to this chapter is translated by the author and was taken from www.mujeractual.com.

1 Ricard Bru, 'Tentacles of Love and Death: From Hokusai to Picasso', in *Imágenes Secretas: Picasso y la estampa erotica japonesa* (Barcelona, 2009), p. 194.
2 Ibid., p. 195.
3 Victor Hugo, *Les Travailleurs de la mer* [1866], quoted in *Imágenes Secretas*, p. 193.
4 Frank Thomas Bullen, *Denizens of the Deep* (New York, 1904), p. 128.
5 Jacques Schnier, 'Morphology of a Symbol: The Octopus', *American Imago*, 13 (1956), pp. 3–31.
6 Henry Lee, *Sea Fables Explained* (London, 1883), p. 51.
7 Henry Lee, *The Octopus; or, the 'Devil-fish' of Fiction and of Fact* (London, 1875), p. 8.
8 Bru, 'Tentacles of Love and Death', pp. 190–91.
9 Gabi Greve, 'Octopus (Tako)', http://worldkigodatabase.blogspot.co.uk, 8 March 2007.
10 Miki Katao, 'Shinkyogoku and Teramachi-dori', Culture and Foods, www.kyopro.kufs.ac.jp/English.htm, accessed 15 June 2013.
11 Ian Reader and George J. Tanabe Jr, *Practically Religious: Worldly Benefits and the Common Religion of Japan* (Honolulu, 1998), p. 249.
12 Terri Saul, 'The Zak Smith Interview', http://quarterlyconversation.com, accessed 31 October 2012.
13 Karmentxu Marín, 'Tengo mucha relación con los pulpos', *El País* (1 May 2011), p. 64, trans. author.

14 Francesca Myman, 'Poulpe Pulps: Vintage Octopus Magazine Covers', http://francesca.net/pulp, accessed 31 October 2012.
15 Roland Anderson, '20,000 Tentacles Under the Sea', *Of Sea and Shore*, XV/2 (1992), pp. 78–84, at www.thecephalopodpage.org/awful, accessed 31 October 2012.
16 Jean Painlevé's *Les Amours de la pieuvre* (*The Love Life of an Octopus*) is available online at www.youtube.com, accessed 31 October 2012.

7 OCTOPUS KEEPING

1 Roy Caldwell (Neogonadactylus), 'Octopus Bites', www.tonmo.com, 16 August 2007.
2 John Roach, 'Newfound Octopus Impersonates Fish, Snakes', http://news.nationalgeographic.com (21 September 2001).
3 Roy Caldwell and Christopher Shaw, 'Mimic Octopuses: Will We Love Them To Death?', www.thecephalopodpage.org, accessed 31 October 2012.
4 Jennifer A. Mather, Roland C. Anderson and James B. Wood, *Octopus: The Ocean's Intelligent Invertebrate* (Portland, OR, 2010), p. 175.
5 Ibid., pp. 175–6.
6 Nancy King, 'So You Want to Keep an Octopus', *Tropical Fish Magazine* (June 2007), at www.tfhmagazine.com.
7 Jennifer A. Mather and Roland C. Anderson, 'Ethics and Invertebrates: A Cephalopod Perspective', *Diseases of Aquatic Organisms*, 75 (2007), pp. 119–26.
8 Roland C. Anderson and Andrea Leontiu, 'Evaluating Toys for Octopuses (*Enteroctopus dofleini*, Cephalopoda)', www.thecephalopodpage.org, accessed 31 October 2012.
9 James B. Wood and Roland C. Anderson, 'Interspecific Evaluation of Octopus Escape Behavior', *Journal of Applied Animal Welfare Science*, VII/2 (2004), pp. 95–106.
10 Henry Lee, *The Octopus; or, the 'Devil-fish' of Fiction and of Fact* (London, 1875), p. 36.

11 Jacques-Yves Cousteau and Philippe Diolé, *Octopus and Squid: The Soft Intelligence* (New York, 1973), p. 41.
12 Lee, *The Octopus*, p. 38.
13 Frank W. Lane, *Kingdom of the Octopus* (New York, 1960), p. 77.
14 Graziano Fiorito, interview with the author, March 2010.
15 Lincoln Stoller, interview with Jerome Lettvin, May 2007, at www.tengerresearch.com.
16 Roy Caldwell, 'What Makes Blue-rings So Deadly? Blue-ringed Octopus have Tetrodotoxin', www.thecephalopodpage.org, accessed 31 October 2012.
17 Carolyn Barry, 'All Octopuses are Venomous, Study Says', www.nationalgeographic.com/news, 17 April 2009.
18 A. Anastasi and V. Erspamer, 'Occurrence and Some Properties of Eledoisin in Extracts of Posterior Salivay Glands of Eledone', *British Journal of Pharmacology*, 19 (1962), pp. 326–36.
19 Charles Derby, 'Escape By Inking and Secreting: Marine Molluscs Avoid Predators through a Rich Array of Chemicals and Mechanisms', *Biological Bulletin*, 213 (2007), pp. 274–89.
20 Cousteau and Diolé, *Octopus and Squid*, p. 72.
21 M. J. Wells, *Octopus: Physiology and Behaviour of an Advanced Invertebrate* (London, 1978), p. 68.
22 Bob Pool, 'Octopus Floods Santa Monica Pier Aquarium', *Los Angeles Times* (27 February 2009).
23 'Mark Wahlberg's Son Attacked By "Giant" Octopus', www.starpulse.com, 6 August 2010.
24 P. R. Boyle, *The UFAW Handbook on the Care and Management of Cephalopods in the Laboratory* (Potters Bar, Hertfordshire, 1991), p. 7.
25 Nicola Nosengo, 'European Directive Gets Its Tentacles into Octopus Research', *Nature* (12 April 2011), at www.nature.com.
26 N. A. Moltschaniwsky et al., 'Ethical and Welfare Considerations When Using Cephalopods as Experimental Animals', *Reviews in Fish Biology and Fisheries*, 17 (2007), pp. 455–76.

Select Bibliography

Anderson, Roland, and Jennifer Mather, 'Octopuses are Smart Suckers!?', www.thecephalopodpage.org, accessed 24 October 2012
Aristotle, *Historia Animalium*, trans. D'Arcy Wentworth Thompson (Oxford, 1910)
Bartsch, Paul, 'Pirates of the Deep: Stories of the Squid and Octopus', *Smithsonian Institute Annual Report for 1916*, pp. 347–75
Bitterman, M. E., *Invertebrate Learning*, ed. William C. Corning (New York, 1975), vol. III
Cousteau, Jacques-Yves, and Philippe Diolé, *Octopus and Squid: The Soft Intelligence* (New York, 1973)
Fiorito, Graziano, and Pietro Scotto, 'Observational Learning in *Octopus vulgaris*', *Science*, 256 (24 April 1992), pp. 545–7
Hanlon, Roger T., and John B. Messenger, *Cephalopod Behaviour* (Cambridge, 1996)
Kiley, Brendan, 'Sexy Beast', www.thestranger.com, 8 September 2009
Lane, Frank, *Kingdom of the Octopus* (New York, 1960)
Lee, Henry, *The Octopus; or, The 'Devil-fish' of Fiction and of Fact* (London, 1875)
Linden, Eugene, *The Octopus and the Orangutan* (New York, 2003)
Mather, Jennifer A., 'To Boldly Go Where No Mollusc has Gone Before: Personality, Play, Thinking and Consciousness in Cephalopods', *American Malocological Bulletin*, 234 (2008), pp. 51–8
—, Roland C. Anderson and Janes B. Wood, *Octopus: The Ocean's Intelligent Invertebrate* (Portland, OR, 2010)

Moynihan, Martin, *Communication and Noncommunication in Cephalopods* (Bloomington, IN, 1985)
Oppian, *Halieutica*, trans. A. W. Mair (Chicago, IL, 1928)
Squire, Larry, ed., *The History of Neuroscience in Autobiography* (San Diego, CA, 2001)
Wells, M. J., *Octopus: Physiology and Behaviour of an Advanced Invertebrate* (London, 1969)
Young, John Z., *The Anatomy of the Nervous System of 'Octopus vulgaris'* (Oxford, 1971)

Associations and Websites

AquacultureHub
www.aquaculturehub.org

Cephalopod Research
www.cephalopodresearch.org

CephBase (database on all living cephalopods)
http://nano.nstl.gov.cn/sea/MirrorResources/6448

The Octopus Group, Hebrew University of Jerusalem
www.octopus.huji.ac.il

The Octopus News Magazine Online
www.tonmo.com

Octopus stock status
www.montereybayaquarium.org

Octopus vulgaris FAO Fact Sheet
www.fao.org/fishery/species/3571/en

Dr James Woods's website
www.thecephalopodpage.org

Acknowledgements

I had a chance to avail myself of some fine libraries while researching this book, and want to thank the staffs of two in particular: the library at the Stazione Zoologica Anton Dohrn in Naples; and the kind and friendly staff at the Instituto de Ciencias del Mar in Barcelona. Thanks also to Dr Roger Villanueva at the same institute in Barcelona, and to Dr Carlos Rosas at the Universidad Nacional Autónoma de México's marine research institute in Sisal, Mexico, and to his wonderful wife Maru Chimal. The six members of the Moluscos del Mayab, the Mayan Mollusc Cooperative, made room for me as a fellow worker at their octopus farm in Sisal, patiently corrected my mistakes, fed me like a king and kept me laughing. *Un abrazo fuerte a* Silvia del Carmen Canul Pardenilla; María Virginia Narcisa Uicab Novelo; Julio Ernesto Sierra Delgado; Juana de la Cruz Maldonado Ek; Antonio Cob Reyes; and Bianca Daniela Hernández Hernández. And thanks to Sofia Burckle for lifting my spirits.

Photo Acknowledgements

The author and publishers wish to express their thanks to the below sources of illustrative material and/or permission to reproduce it. (Some locations uncredited in the captions for reasons of brevity are also given below.)

Photo Aflo/Rex Features: p. 97; photo annej/BigStockPhoto: p. 43; photos by author: pp. 29 (foot), 89, 156; Bibliothèque Nationale de France, Paris: p. 130; courtesy of the artist (Benedetta Bonichi): p. 17; courtesy of the artist (Gloria Bornstein): p. 170; photo Bournemouth News/Rex Features: p. 54; the British Museum, London: pp. 19, 84, 91, 94, 96 (top), 113, 136; photos © The Trustees of the British Museum, London: pp. 19, 41, 84, 91, 94, 96 (top), 98, 113, 128, 129, 136, 141; photo Tom Campbell/SplashdownDirect/Rex Features: p. 12; photo Becky Dayhuff, courtesy NOAA: p. 37; photo M. Evans/Newspix/Rex Features: p. 54; photo EXTREME-PHOTOGRAPHER/2013 iStock International Inc.: p. 45; photo F1 Online/Rex Features: p. 34; photo FernandoAH/2013 iStock International Inc.: p. 104; photo Fisheries and Oceans Canada/Rex Features: p. 13; photo Angelo Giampiccolo/bluegreenpictures.com/Rex Features: p. 38; courtesy of the artist (Donna Glassford): p. 152; photo Mark Harding/SplashdownDirect/Rex Features: p. 20; photo holbox/BigStockPhoto: p. 36; photo holgs/2013 iStock International Inc.: p. 117; photo Image Source/Rex Features: p. 18; photo jalbersmead: p. 26 (foot); photo Jman78/2013 iStock International Inc.: p. 81; from Henry Lee, *The Octopus; or, The 'Devil-Fish' of Fiction and of Fact* (London, 1875): pp. 23, 123, 135; photos Library of Congress,

Washington, DC (Prints and Photographs Division): pp. 31, 134, 138, 145, 147, 148, 163, 166; Los Angeles County Museum of Art: p. 118; from Richard Lydekker, *The Royal Natural History*, vol. VI (London, 1896): p. 41; photo Dwayne Meadows, NOAA/NMFS/OPR: p. 10; photo Mike T/BigStockPhoto: p. 32 (foot); from Gustav Mützel, *Die Gartenlaube* (Leipzig, 1894): p. 59; courtesy Naples Zoological Station: pp. 49, 50; Natural History Museum, London: p. 66; photo Nature Picture Library/ Rex Features: p. 165; photo Steve Nicklas, courtesy NOAA: p. 150; photo courtesy NOAA: p. 174; photo NOAA/Monterey Bay Aquarium Research Institute: p. 46; photo norme/2013 iStock International Inc.: p. 100; photo oversnap/2013 iStock International Inc.: p. 107; photo Pacific-Klaus: p. 70; photo Constantinos Petrinos/Nature Picture Library/ Rex Features: p. 44; photo piola666/2013 iStock International Inc.: p. 6; photo pipehorse/BigStockPhoto: p. 21; photo Rex Features: p. 108; photo rie/BigStockPhoto: p. 111; photo Rixie/BigStockPhoto: p. 92; photos Roger-Viollet/Rex Features: pp. 11, 137; photos Jeff Rotman/ Nature Picture Library/Rex Features: pp. 30, 39, 40; photo rudisill/ 2013 iStock International Inc.: p. 121; photo Jose B. Ruiz/Nature Picture Library/Rex Features: p. 32 (top); photos Sipa Press/Rex Features: p. 153; photo stefan kerkhofs/BigStockPhoto: p. 15; photo SUNSET/Rex Features: p. 71; photo tirc83/2013 iStock International Inc.: pp. 22; photo Mark Tworkowski/Solent News/Rex Features: p. 26 (top); from *The United States Marines* [children's magazine], 3 (1944): p. 149; from Jules Verne, *Twenty Thousand Leagues Under the Sea*: p. 150; photo vlas2002/BigStockPhoto: p. 96 (foot); Voroneţ Monastery, Romania: p. 9; photo Werner Forman Archive/private collection: p. 132; photo Daniel Wiedemann/BigStockPhoto: p. 27; photo Dennis Wile: p. 152; photo Matt Wilson/Jay Clark, NOAA/NMFS/AFSC: p. 29 (top); photo Zoological Society of London: p. 41.

Index

Addams, Charles 151
Aelianus, Claudius 16
Akashi (Japan) 116, 118
Aldrovandi, Ulisse 134
Anderson, Roland 69–73, 146–7, 158–60
Apicius, Marcus Gavius 109
aquaculture 99–103
Aristotle, *History of Animals* 16, 47–8, 90–91

Barceló, Miguel 144
Bartsch, Paul 107
Bashō, Matsuo 80
Beardsley, Aubrey 127
Binichi, Benedetta, *The Pearl Necklace* 17
Bitterman, Jeff 68
blue-ringed octopus 70, 164, *165*
Boal, Jean 75–8
Bond, James 143
Bornstein, Gloria *170*
Boycott, Brian B. 54–6
Boyle, Peter 170–71
Buhot, Félix, *Le Peintre de Marine 41*
Bull, Charles Livingston *31*

Caldwell, Roy 155, 157, 164
Canary Islands 80, 85
Catania fish market, Sicily *112*
Caule, Pierre 143
Chifflart, François-Nicolas, *The Monster 11*
Clearchus of Soli 16
Coates, C. W. 161
Corman, Roger 145
Cousteau, Jacques 65, 160
 Octopus and Squid: The Soft Intelligence 7
 octopus bites 167
Cutrone, Vincent 119–20, 122, 124
cuttlefish 77–8

Dakhla 82–3, 85–7
Dalby, Andrew, *Food in the Ancient World: From A To Z* 106–7
 octopus beating 119
Darwin, Charles 48

Dews, Peter 60–62
Dilly, Peter 68
Diogenes 108–9
Disney, Walt 149–51, 153
Dohrn, Anton 48–51, *50*, 161–2

Easter Island rock carving *88*
Enteroctopus dofleini (giant Pacific octopus) 12, *39*, 71, 73, 160, 168

Fidalgo Santamariña, José Antonio 111
Fiorito, Graziano 64–9, 78–9
fishing
  in Dakhla 83–7
  in Japan 95–9
  in the Mediterranean 90–94
  with pots 28, 30, *32*
  in the Yucatán 87–90
Flamen, Albert 113
Fry, Brian 165

Galicia 111–12
Glassford, Donna, *The Distance To the Moon* 152
Goncourt, Edmond de 127
Gras, Pere Pau 114
Greek coin with octopus *91*
Green, W. Kirby 113–14

Hanlon, Roger 7, 11, 13
Hawaiian octopus fishing lure *84*
Henry, Pierre 148
Hochman, Benyamin 78–9

Hokkei, Toyota *166*
Hokusai, Katsushika, *The Dream of the Fisherman's Wife* 126, 128, *128*, 138, 146
Hugo, Victor, *The Toilers of the Sea* 11, 126, 129–32, *130*, 138
Huysmans, Joris-Karl 128

Japan
  octopus beating 119
  octopus consumption 95–7
  octopus cooking 118–19
  octopus fishery 97, 99

King, Nancy 158–9
Klimt, Gustav 127, 143
Kuniyoshi, Utagawa *141*
Kyōsai, Kawanabe *138*

Lane, Frank, *Kingdom of the Octopus* 30–31, 161
Landa, Diego de, *An Account of the Things of Yucatán* 105
Lee, Henry, *The Octopus* 16, 113, 123, 134, *134*, 138, 160–61
Lettvin, Jerome 162
Llibre de Sent Soví 109
Llibre del coch 110
Linden, Eugene, *The Octopus and the Orangutan* 64
Lydekker, Richard, *Cephalopoda* 42

Marine Biological Laboratory 7
Mather, Jennifer 44–6, 69–70,

72–5, 76, 77, 78–9, 158–9
mimic octopus 156–7, *157*
Minoan period 10
    octopus frieze *110*
Morocco
    octopus fishery 81–7
Moynihan, Martin 18

nautilus 12, 14, 47
Nosengo, Nicola 172

O Carballiño festival, Spain 113
observational learning 64, 66–7
octopus
    activity 43–6
    arms 33–5, *45*
    blood 19–20
    brain 48
    chromatophores 18–19
    colour-blindness 35–6
    digestion 43
    eggs 24–7, *27*
    hectocotylus 21
    ink 33
    larvae 27–8, *29*
    venom 28, 41, 164–6
Octopus bimaculoides (California two-spot octopus) 160, *163*
Octopus maya (Mayan octopus) 28
    aquaculture 101–3
    babies *29*
    bites *156*
    fisheries 87–90
    flavour of 105

Octopus vulgaris (common octopus) *21*, 61, 68, 81, 87, 90, 160, *169*
    aquaculture 99–100
    as prey 20
    bites 167
    eye *37*
    gazing at 7
    global demand for 83
    on a reef *38*
    Paul the Octopus 153, *153*
    suckers *23*
    flavour of 103, 105–6
Oppian of Corycus 91

Painlevé, Jean 147–8
Philoxenu of Leucas 107
Picasso, Pablo 126–7, 153
Pliny the Elder 91, 107, 109
Pompeii 9, 136
Portugal
    octopus fishery 81
prey 37, 40, *40*
Pynchon, Thomas 143, 145

Rabal i Merola, Victòria *142*
radula 40–41
reproduction 21–4
Ripert, Eric 124–5
Rosas, Carlos 102

saltwater aquariums 158
Scappi, Bartolomeo 110–11
Schiller, Paul 53
Schliemann, Heinrich 136

Schnier, Jacques 133–4
senescence 24–7, 153
Seto Inland Sea 97, 114–15
shunga 126–7, *129*
Silurian period 14
Skinner, B. F. 60
Smith, Zak 143–4
Spain
    octopus fishery 81, 83
Starr, Ringo 28
Stazione Zoologica Anton
    Dohrn 48–54, *49*, 64–5, 162

Taishokan 138, 146–7
tako 115–6, 139
takoyaki 116, *117*
tentacle sex 139–40
tetrodotoxin 164
Theognis of Megara 16
Tomekichi, Endo 116
Toulouse-Lautrec, Henri de 127

Wahlberg, Mark 168–9
Wells, H. G. 9
Wells, Martin J. 9, 14, 57–60
    and octopus bites 167
Wodinsky, Jerome 25, 41
Wood, James 160

Young, John Z. 53–60
    The Anatomy of the Nervous
    System of 'Octopus vulgaris' 47

Zola, Émile 127